20/20 VISIONS

20/20 VISIONS

The Futures of Christianity in Britain

Bernard Crick   Monica Furlong   Adrian Hastings   Kim Knott
Barry Rogerson   John J Vincent   Andrew Walker

Edited by
HADDON WILLMER

First published in Great Britain 1992
SPCK
Holy Trinity Church
Marylebone Road
London NW1 4DU

British Library Cataloguing-in-Publication Data

A catalogue record for this book is available from the
British Library

ISBN 0 281 04560 7

Typeset by Latimer Trend & Co Ltd, Plymouth
Printed in Great Britain by The Longdunn Press, Bristol

Contents

Contributors

HADDON WILLMER had a radical evangelical Free Church upbringing, which taught him the Bible as well as opening his eyes to the relevance of Machiavelli to the study of religion. After National Service in which he saw Jerusalem and Baghdad, he learnt church history and theology in Cambridge under great liberal Anglicans like Geoffrey Lampe. He has worked in the Department of Theology and Religious Studies in the University of Leeds since 1966. He is an active but ecumenical Baptist layperson and preacher.

BERNARD CRICK is Emeritus Professor of Politics at Birkbeck College, University of London. Since 1984 he has lived in Edinburgh and is an Honorary Fellow of the University. His two main works are *In Defence of Politics*, which has been in print since 1962, and *George Orwell: A Life*. In 1974 he gave the Voltaire Memorial Lectures for the British Humanist Association, published as *Crime, Rape and Gin*, which he called a political philosopher's reflections on violence, pornography and drug addiction. An Honorary Associate of the British Humanists, he has also campaigned for balanced political education in schools, and for universities to admit more part-timers and mature students.

MONICA FURLONG is a former Fleet Street feature writer, and BBC producer. She is the author of biographies of Thomas Merton, Alan Watts and Thérèse of Lisieux, several books about contemplative spirituality, two adult novels, and, most recently, two children's novels, *Wise Child* and *A Year and a Day*, set in the Dark Ages. She is working on a third book in the same series. She holds an honorary doctorate in divinity from the General Theological Seminary, New York. She is a Christian feminist, and a former moderator of the Movement for the Ordination of Women. She lives in West London.

ADRIAN HASTINGS studied history at Oxford and theology in Rome. He worked in Uganda, Tanzania and Zambia between 1958 and 1970, was lecturer and reader in Religious Studies, University of Aberdeen, 1976–82, Professor of Religious Studies, University of Zimbabwe, 1982–5 and, since 1985, Professor of Theology at the University of Leeds. Among his recent publications are *A History of English Christianity, 1920–1990* (SCM 1991), *African Catholicism* (SCM 1989), *The Theology of a Protestant Catholic* (SCM 1990), *Robert Runcie* (Mowbray 1991) and *Church and State: The English Experience* (University of Exeter Press 1991). He is the editor of *Modern Catholicism: Vatican II and After* (SPCK 1991).

KIM KNOTT has lived and worked in Leeds for eighteen years, first as a student, latterly as a researcher and lecturer in the Department of Theology and Religious Studies. She has written two books and a number of articles on contemporary religions, particularly Hinduism, and her current creative work includes researching a book on recent developments in the religions of Britian's Asian communities, writing on women and religion, and, most significantly, having her first baby.

BARRY ROGERSON worked for the Midland Bank and did his National Service as a radar instructor before studying theology at the University of Leeds. He trained at Wells Theological College and, after two curacies in the Diocese of Durham, taught at both Lichfield and Salisbury and Wells Theological Colleges. He became the first Bishop of Wolverhampton after being team rector of a Black Country parish. It was during this time that he was chairman of the Inter-Faith Consultancy Group. In 1985 he became Bishop of Bristol. He is chairman of the Advisory Board of Ministry, a member of the Faith and Order Commission of the World Council of Churches, and chairman of the Melanesian Mission.

JOHN J. VINCENT completed a doctorate on discipleship with Oscar Cullmann and Karl Barth in Basel, and has since been a Methodist minister in Wythenshawe, Rochdale, and (since 1970) Sheffield. He has been a prominent figure in radical Christian movements throughout his ministry. In 1967 he helped form the Ashram Community, and in 1970 the Sheffield Inner City Ecumenical Mission and the Urban Theology Unit. He was president of the Methodist Conference, 1989–90. His books include *Into the City* (Epworth 1982), *Radical Jesus* (Marshall Pickering 1986), *Mark at Work* (with J.D. Davies, Bible Reading Fellowship 1986), *Britain in the 90's* (Methodist Publishing House 1989), *Gospel in the 90's* (Methodist Publishing House 1990), and *Discipleship in the 90's* (Methodist Publishing House 1991).

ANDREW WALKER is lecturer in theology and education at King's College, University of London. He is also the director of the C. S. Lewis Centre for the study of religion and modernity and visiting professor at Perkins School of Theology, Southern Methodist University. With a background in social science, Andrew Walker now concentrates on Christianity and modern culture. He is the author of *Restoring the Kingdom: The Radical Christianity of the House Church Movement* (Hodder & Stoughton 1988) and editor of *Different Gospels: Christian orthodoxy and modern theologies* (Hodder & Stoughton 1988).

Acknowledgements

These essays were sponsored by the Department of Theology and Religious Studies at the University of Leeds. Special thanks for indispensable help are due to Ingrid Lawrie, who oversaw all arrangements for the essays and the preparation of the book, and to Jill Killington, who created posters, organized publicity, and typed manuscripts.

INTRODUCTION

HADDON WILLMER

- How will Christianity in Britain change over the next thirty years?
- Why will it change in the ways you expect?
- How do the changes you expect fit with the changes you would like to see?
- How should we cope with the tension between what we expect and what we would like?

These questions are the seeds of this book. The authors were asked to 'bear them in mind' when they prepared their contributions to a series of Open Lectures at the University of Leeds in 1991. No-one expected direct answers, and all knew there could not be simple information concerning the future. The questions are more like subjects for rumination and we wanted to overhear what happens inside the thinking of those who 'bear them in mind'.

Thinking thirty years ahead about Christianity in Britain – or anything else – is like driving in fog. We assume the road will be there waiting for us when we get to it: but we see very little and we cannot know for sure that the road will go on being navigable. Safety requires more vision than is given. Because of the danger, some people crawl along or even give up the journey. Those who have to travel will strain their eyes trying to decipher objects and impressions misshapen by the fog: one minute the car in front is clearly visible, and the next it has been obscured from us in a cloud. We cannot be sure that anything is really what it seems. We lose perspective and sense of distance. The brain is overstretched; normally it reads what is happening on the road without frantic calculation, but in fog it gropes to interpret elusive and maybe illusory evidence, much of which may be irrelevant, accidental shimmerings of stray light on the mist. It is easy to get confused, disoriented. Concentration is difficult when there is nothing but vague and uncertain shapes to respond to. Always it is easier to see the reflection of one's own headlamps than any hard objects cloaked in fog.

It is no wonder, then, that some of the experienced authors whose work appears here confessed that they had found the task not only interesting, but extraordinarily difficult. Taking 2020 as the horizon exacerbates the problem. If we are asked about the near future, say 1993 or 1994, we can give plausible answers by surveying what is already going on. Next year may indeed surprise us with the totally unexpected, but there is a good chance that what happens then will be an intelligible development of the present. We can know the people, powers and imaginations already at work in shaping next year, and few of them will have the flexibility to change course drastically in a few months. Our concept of the short-term future is shaped by what we are already busy with. The demand to look twenty-five years ahead, or to 2020, however, requires us to venture into the unknown, and to concentrate on the unknowable.

The year 2020 elongates our view to the point where it goes beyond what we can plan or confidently extrapolate from the present. Imagination rooted in present reality peters out and is replaced by artificial fantasy, disconnected from our apparently solid experience. The year 2020 will be the day of the next generation, or even of our grandchildren, and we find it hard to imagine what their imagination will bring forth and what material it might have to work upon. We may be tempted not to care about 2020, because we can do so little about it and, by then, many of us will no longer be making history. But children and grandchildren may entice us to care.

What, then, is the use of being concerned about the distant future? How is interest in it to be justified? Does talking about the distant future appeal only to the intellectual equivalent of the dare-devil driver? Within a university or a self-respecting community of faith, is pondering on the future inevitably an indisciplined activity without serious claim on attention? In the face of such questions, it may be helpful to assess what can be achieved by thinking about Christianity 'towards 2020'.

REMEMBERING

Looking towards 2020 does not imply abandoning the past. Concern with the future reawakens interest in the past, though not for its own sake or as a refuge from the present. Different possibilities in the future will generate different readings of the past. Without future-orientation, we slide into idolizing the past, through stubborn defence of traditions or through nostalgia, a mood in which the future is felt merely as a threat to the beloved refuge of the past. Enquiring about the future cannot make us experts in the history of what has not yet happened, but it will spur us to read the past in new ways. The historically minded Christian should not fear the invitation to look into the future; interest in the future revives investigation of our pasts.

PREDICTING

The question of the future would appear to be an invitation to predict. Sensible people and disciplined scholars shy away from prediction: the observed failure rate is too high. In part, this book challenges people to take that risk. When we asked 'What do you think will happen?', we were requiring an element of prediction. But directing attention to the future does not imply that we can know the future as we think we know the past. No amount of scholarship or methodological sophistication can dissolve the fog that shrouds the future. There are no 'facts' to be collected. The attempt to predict is therefore a necessary device or idiom in any serious talk of the future, but prediction is not what talk of the future achieves. So it cannot be its essential purpose. In the study of the future, prediction is subordinated to and relativized by other activities.

PRAYING

Convincing or useful talk of the future is, in part, like prayer: it is the articulation of wishes by people who are growing in self-understanding, responsibility and faith. They grow partly through experiences in which what actually happens often does not accord with their wishes. Is the best prayer without content, and thus without a serious interest in whether the future will turn out one way or another? Is prayer a glad resignation of ourselves and all things to God, regardless of what actually happens? Is the true reward of prayer, the end it seeks, a participation in God that makes us indifferent to the future? It is not so with a prayer like Jesus' in Gethsemane: 'Father, take this cup from me. Nevertheless not my will, but yours be done.' That prayer is wrestling with an awareness of what is going to happen. It is prayer with future preferences. That prayer's surrender to God only has significance because it is made in the context of a readiness to live through a future perceived to be full of threats of pain, loss and disaster. Nowadays, academic theology is renewing its links with prayer and spirituality, but it may be in danger of attending onesidedly to the kinds of prayer that seek timelessness. To focus on the future is to bring historical action and responsibility back into prayer in a serious way.

VENTURING

The prayer of Gethsemane reminds us how personal the question of the future is. In it the identity of persons and communities is at stake, for through wishing and enduring the future they make themselves in time, one way or another. The future is the stage given to people and

4

communities on which they can present and project themselves, choosing to try out or essay definite personal and communal identities from an infinity of possibilities. Each person only lives one life, although any life can be at least imagined as having many options. Any life has its crises and stages; at each turning point or new opening, people may essay a new self, a new way; but however many ways we try out, a lifetime's attempts amount only to a fraction of the possibilities. Identity is not simply given: we discover it by venturing into the future.

In this process, we come to know ourselves better as we observe how we set about seeing the future and making it. Thus the invitation to think towards the future is a way to self-knowledge or to knowledge of others: we know who they are, not just by looking at their pedigree but at their prospects. People and groups are not defined completely by their pasts: they become themselves in making their futures; and in the processes of that future-making, they find the pasts from which they live and want to live.

Christianity, by the same token, is not just what it has been and is now, but also what it is capable of in the future. To recognize and maintain the identity of Christianity is a proper responsibility as well as an improper worry for Christians. It cannot be discharged by looking only to the past. Christian identity is not merely given: like the Promised Land, it has to be entered. It is what pilgrims find, not what inheritors possess.

PLANNING

Is the future to be planned? In today's usage of the word, planning involves the combination of prediction and the will, with the help of power, to realize the prediction. Christianity lives from too many hearts, in too many situations, it is too complex and pluralist to be significantly plannable. Nevertheless, religious organizations, especially if they are self-consciously modern and efficient, have plans and planners. Church growth, for example, can be a planning science, at least in the way it carries out investigations and presents some of its results. But even the most meticulous planning has to allow for the Holy Spirit, free as the wind, and the unmanageable moods of people. Some things we can plan with a fair chance of making them happen, while in other wider developments there is too much slippage between plan and performance. We might conclude that the future of a religion in 2020 cannot be planned, but people will incessantly plan for the future, partly by giving themselves a dual-track preparation, being ready both for the expected and for surprises. The predictive element in planning can never be more than provisional; the solid element in planning is the act by which we take responsibility and give ourselves intelligently to the risks and opportunities of the future. Thus the future we can plan is as much inside ourselves as outside. Once more we see that the enquiry into planning the futures of Christianity leads us to reckon with the kinds of people and communities we are. With what spirit, values and understanding do we go forward into the future? What are we open to and what are we closed against? What can we welcome and use positively, if it comes our way, and what threatens and inhibits us?

So speaking of the future will bring into the open what people care about and what inspires them. In short, it helps us to know ourselves, individually and corporately.

THE FUTURE IN ACADEMIC THEOLOGY AND RELIGIOUS STUDIES

Most theology – like most human action – is moved and directed by hopes, fears and calculations about the future. Little research on the past is done without some feeling, however obscure, that the chosen historical subject will be significant for the present. Sometimes people seek a piece of the past, to be resurrected through research, which will be like home in the present. Sometimes, a section of the past is investigated because it seems likely to illuminate choices that have to be made in the present. Sometimes some strand of the past is felt to deserve to have a future: the historian or the historically minded theologian is like a warden of endangered species. Though in all these ways academic theology is often future-oriented, there is no discipline of theological futurology and no concerted attempt to manage the intellectual and moral difficulties of such an enterprise. Academic theology should be more explicit about the fears, hopes and loves that inspire it; to be frank here is a condition of being scientific. Study is scientific only as it shows its working and does not simply state its conclusions like an oracle. A scientific approach attends as much to its methods as to its content; and that requires it consciously to take account of the effects of the thinker and the thinking community on what is thought. Therefore it is essential to bring to light the inspirations and inhibitions that affect the performance of theologians and thinking believers generally. Theological education that does not call students to be critically and confidently aware of the dimensions of hope and fear in their own work is intellectually, as well as morally, weak.

POLICY

I hope – I do not know whether all the writers here would agree – that our essays might encourage a new emphasis in theology and religious studies, in which these disciplines would be more explicit in discussing their essential future-orientations and in developing themselves in the light of that awareness. Conversation about futures needs to be raised intellectually from the level of idle fancy, partisan apologia or wild talk to be indulged in the pub at the end of a day's serious study. New disciplines, new methods, may be in the making here. For example, the systematic study of church policy needs to be fostered. Church policy necessarily deals both with the mundane management and finance of religious communities and with their spiritual quests, theology and service. Schleiermacher wanted the theoretical and practical sides of theology to be balanced.[1]

When the balance broke down, he thought the cultivation of the knowledge of Christianity produced the 'theologian, in the narrower sense' while concern with 'church government' was left to the 'clergyman'. The outcome would be the too-familiar tension between academic theology and church. Schleiermacher looked for the two functions to be practised harmoniously, as he expected they would be by the sort of person he called 'the prince of the church'.

Can we now look for theology and religious studies that will nurture princes? Or does the idea alienate us, suggesting that academic theology would only be of use to bishops (and their equivalents) and those who were in training to be bishops? It need not put us off: the task of being princes – and princesses – of the Church is now democratized in a way unthinkable to Schleiermacher. The challenge is serious. Too much theological education seems to be directed towards producing scholars who are happiest looking backwards and perhaps inwards and upwards. And when there is a revolt against such theology, it frequently falls into a practical short-termism of the pastor and the church-manager. The prince or princess of the Church looks forward, because he or she has to conceive of theology not just as theory, but as faithful policy-making in the service of the gospel.

If the study of future-oriented church policy is to be developed in secular and pluralist universities, it will have to be done in the context of a wider discipline that investigates policy as a mode of being religious in all faiths. Such a discipline would bring together many different kinds of study: historical, theological, sociological and ethical.

CHRISTIANITY IN PLURALIST BRITAIN

A question that not surprisingly engages some of the writers here is why special attention should be given to the futures of Christianity in Britain. The question is sharpened if we look to a pluralist future in an open and comparative way.

One reason for looking at Britain in this way is that Christianity has been of enormous significance for the historical development of British society, culture and values. Arguably it still is, and will be, though in what ways is unclear. The futures – the plural is deliberate and necessary – of Christianity are not of interest to Christians alone: people in Britain who are of other religions and those who prefer to do without religion have proper concerns with what will happen to Christianity. Sometimes they may take notice of it in order to protect themselves. One way or another, they will certainly contribute to the futures of Christianity. Kim Knott especially draws attention to their voices.

Another reason for being interested in the futures of Christianity in Britain (not, note, British Christianities) is that the next thirty years could bring more rapid and fundamental change than we have seen hitherto. Will Christianity have much of a public future, or will secularization continue to privatize it? Is privatized Christianity capable of saving itself from becoming trivial? Is the horizon of the future of Christianity in Britain its possible disappearance? That event is imaginable, though not probable; but the idea is enough to infuse an apocalyptic thrill into the discussion. The possibility of the dissolution of Christianity's traditional public presence in British society will variously arouse or depress Christian communities and affect their policy-making. Some fear and mourn its end; others are evidently less worried, judging that, if Christianity fades, other vehicles are available for the spiritual and cultural quests it has carried in its time. Would a change of vehicle make much difference?

BRITAIN AND ENGLAND

The territorial targeting of this book is blurred. The essays were originally planned to deal with the futures of Christianity in England. We found that this restriction could not consistently be observed. Adrian Hastings and Monica Furlong, for example, speak in different idioms, but share a world-embracing global perspective. Barry Rogerson includes Europe in his view. Bernard Crick draws on experience of British–Irish relationships and puts England in its place by emphasizing the pluralism of nationalities within British history, while Kim Knott discusses some transforming implications of inter-faith relations for the future of Christianity, now that many faiths of the world are at home in Britain. Thus in practice it was discovered that one cannot talk about England without talking about Britain – and much more than Britain.

Less now than ever has Christianity in Britain the chance of an insular future. It is exposed to and formed by contributions from all over the world. So long as North American Christianity retains its missionary zeal and financial strength, it will continue to invade, and to borrow from, Britain. Europe, East and West, will in the next generation become more important for British Christianity, Catholic and Protestant, than it has been for many years, perhaps for centuries. It is possible that Third World Christianity will have a major impact on British Christianity, though that will depend on British Christians thinking it important to empower Third World Christians to come to Britain in significant numbers as partners in mission. British Christians will have to spend more than money to do that – they will have to renew old sorts of openness to the world and grow new ones.

If British Christianity cannot be insulated from the world, even less can English Christianities be separated from British and Irish Christianities. The Irish, Scots and Welsh have the English language as their own (though not always their only) tongue. They are England's nearest neighbours who, over the centuries, have shared many things with England. Geography has not afforded them adequate protection from the pains of the relationship.

Within the context of Christianity in Britain and Ireland, each of the Christianities of the different parts of Britain and Ireland deserves attention in itself. However much they interact, co-operate and grow together, their continuing differences deserve to be understood. In principle, therefore, Christianity in England might usefully be isolated as a theme, not simply for the English, or for those who live and work in England, but also for those neighbours of England who want to understand what they are faced with. The neighbours of England in Britain and Ireland are relatively much smaller (the population of England is around 47 million, while that of Scotland is 5.1; of Wales 2.8; of Northern Ireland 1.5 and of the Republic of Ireland 3.5 million). They are massively affected by England. England, by contrast, can be indifferent to all but the most extreme forms of pressure from her neighbours. There is a standing inequality in the relation, even when there is great friendship.

There might be another reason for focusing on England within the context of Britain. Christianity is not the same in all the countries of Britain and Ireland. There are shared traditions and common problems, like secularization and pluralism, but there are great differences even in what is held in common. England's Christian traditions are more pluralist and more secularized than is the case with its neighbours. Are they under unhelpful pressure to define themselves protectively against English influence, which is powerful at least because it is big? England has long been felt by many of its Celtic neighbours, not without reason, to be a religious and cultural threat to their traditions and values. Some think 'grey cosmopolitanism' is the result of England's blinkered commercialism and complacent pluralism, which borders on indifference to particular living traditions. Knowing about England's Christianities is at least a prophylactic.

Nevertheless, there is no systematic concentration on England in this book. It is largely concerned with issues that everyone in Britain faces, with local variations. We would not pretend that justice has been done to the futures of all British Christianities, coming, as they do, out of the interactions of many national and denominational and free-wheeling sorts of Christianity. This book opens up the subject: it does not exhaust it.

These essays interact with each other in many different ways. Some intellectually playful readers may like to buy an extra copy of the book, split it apart, and rearrange the chapters in a variety of sequences. The order in which they stand here is not the only rational or illuminating possibility. There are recurring themes and preoccupations, showing what Christians and others must work through together in their futures. Religious pluralism and identity, especially as it is raised by the relations of Christianity, Islam and secularity, is one such theme. Other questions are: Who are the people who will make the people's Church – the poor, the charismatics, the clerics? What will be the social, political and cultural functions of Christianity in the Britain of 2020? What is the significance for Christianity of university departments of theology and religious studies? What does the the Decade of Evangelism mean, and should we be frightened of it? What is the heart of Christian faith and how will it be found in Britain in the future?

NOTE

1 F. Schleiermacher, *Brief Outline on the Study of Theology*, tr. T.N. Tice, Atlanta, John Knox Press, 1965, p. 21.

CHAPTER ONE

All Change

The Presence of the Past in British Christianity

ADRIAN HASTINGS

A NEW AGE BEGINS

In his one indisputable masterpiece, *Let Dons Delight*, variations on a theme in an Oxford common-room, Ronald Knox recounted the conversation of a group of dons once every fifty years in a rather insignificant college named Simon Magus. The first of the conversations takes place in 1588 as they await the Spanish Armada and suspect it will win, the last in 1938, the year Knox wrote the book, which was published the following February. In 1688 the dons were discussing James II's recatholicization of the university and anticipating that it would go still further. It didn't. The 1788 chapter, to the contrary, entitled 'The Unchanging World', presented a group of academics blissfully unaware that the French Revolution was just around the corner. At the end of it all we hear this final conversation:

ROBERTS: Of course, it doesn't really signify much. Because after all the next world war is scheduled to break out in July, isn't it? And after that Drechsel will have his revolution and we shall all have to toe the line. No use quarrelling with the inevitable.

MORDAUNT: Is anything inevitable? If you come to think of it, the fellows of Simon Magus, just three hundred and fifty years ago, must have thought the Armada was going to win, and it never did. Two hundred and fifty years ago, they must have expected England to go Papist again, and it never did.

DRECHSEL: Yes, and a hundred and fifty years ago, they weren't expecting anything to happen; and by God, didn't it?
MASSINGHAM: Well, anyhow, it shews it's a mug's game, prophesying.

Knox here, through the mouth of Roberts, actually predicted the date of the Second World War pretty closely, and even in regard to the revolution that would follow the war and the need to 'toe the line' in Drechsel's coming socialist state, he was not entirely wide of the mark. However, I suspect that Knox himself did not actually expect these things to happen, and was really offering Roberts as yet another example of false prophecy. It wasn't. Yet Mordaunt was right at once to challenge Roberts's capitulation to the inevitable. One's predictions may prove correct, but that does not make them inevitable. There are always alternative futures. Once one starts discussing the future one is in a way prophesying and, in Massingham's words, that seems 'a mug's game'. If so, we are all mugs. The seemingly inevitable, even the outstandingly probable, so often does not happen. Some quite unpredictable factor forces its way to the centre of a well-arranged stage and changes the whole nature of the play. Yet planning is impossible without anticipation, and anticipation means prophesying of a sort. Only mugs don't do it. Perhaps indeed only the very strangest of prophets may tell one to live wholly in the present, to leave tomorrow's cares to tomorrow's carers. For the rest of us, in both world and Church as we stand today, not to attempt to predict the likely shape of tomorrow would be criminally dangerous. But to read the future with any chance at all of success must require a very imaginative handling indeed of the present and the past.

The fleeting knife-edge of the present irremediably divides two endlessly extensive but non-existent realities – future and past. The past grows ever longer and we know always more about it, yet its paradoxical nature is not to be, only to have been, and so now to be in its ultimate objectivity beyond all influence. In its objectivity we cannot control one hair of its head. Yet if its control of us is partly through the sheer way it has been, it also greatly controls us through our perception of it, a perception ever changing. That perception we do greatly control. We can rewrite history, honestly or dishonestly, and many will come to believe even the most dishonest of rewritings. We live then with the past very largely not as it really was, but as in the fleeting knife-edge of the present we perceive it to be. Yet through that perception, in reflection, extension or counter-action, we have to form our still more hazy perception of the coming years.

There were times, many times, in the distant past when people expected the next thirty years to be very little different from the past thirty years, and they were right to do so. Anyone living, for instance, in Britain in 1720 or 1730 or 1740 was in such a time. Change there surely was but rather little and remarkably contained within the public structure of things as given. Such was the period of Walpole's ministry. Move to 1780 and the expectations of most people will not have been much different. They will not have included all that was about to alter in consequence of the French Revolution, the early Industrial Revolution, even the American Revolution, let alone the Evangelical Movement, the early missionary movement, the Romantic Movement, the hastening imperialization of Britain. Yet together these revolutions, movements or whatever, constituted a sea-change, political, cultural, economic and religious, occurring in the thirty years after the 1780s, a hinge time for the modern world. From then on a preoccupation with change grew, and if stability had been a note of eighteenth century consciousness, improvement, the ordered forward march of progress, was a dominant note of the nineteenth century. But it remained a controlled, mostly foreseeable march, possessing something of the predictability of the railway line that is still a fair interpretative model for the Victorian age.

Predictability only really disappears again with the twentieth century. Nobody in 1900 could well have predicted the state of things in 1930; nor in 1930 could they have done so for 1960. In each case, of course, a world war had intervened, but I doubt whether in 1960 many of us could have got the picture anything like right for 1990. Certainly people expected changes at all these dates, but what came was not what they had expected. At other, more cataclysmic, dates, they knew that they didn't know any more what would come, except that it would be different: 1790, 1914, 1940. At such times people felt themselves to be at a hinge of history, and tended indeed to overdo the contrast they made between future and past.

There has never been a time in recorded British history when some degree of significant change was not taking place, but it is a truism to say that the speed of recognizable change has increased pretty steadily and that, as the twentieth century has advanced, it has become both more rapid and more unpredictable – the key agents being now technological knowledge, population growth and mobility, and a disturbed ecological environment. To these, most else is somehow a response. Yet, paradoxically, it is also true that we have just experienced a relatively long period of apparent surface stability. Never since the eighteenth century has a single British Prime Minister governed the country for an entire decade. The political and ideological consistency of Thatcher's Britain was matched by that of the United States of Reagan and Bush, the Germany of Kohl, the France of Mitterrand. Even ecclesiastically, the 1980s presented an unchanging image with John Paul II as Pope, Robert Runcie as Archbishop of Canterbury, Basil Hume as Cardinal Archbishop of Westminster. Moreover, politically and ideologically, there has been very little serious challenge to the current orthodoxy. The moderated socialism of the Western Europe of the post-war years seemed simply to crumble as a coherent and persuasive orthodoxy for society. Its rationale and its enthusiasts withered. One cannot deny that this happened with remarkable speed after Carol Wojtyla became Pope in 1978, Margaret Thatcher replaced Jim Callaghan in 10 Downing Street in 1979, and Ronald Reagan won the presidential election to replace Jimmy Carter in

1980. Even the British Labour Party has finally revamped itself in the toned-down colours of a discreet Thatcherism. The year 1979 may properly then be seen as a hinge year for British history, when the post-war Butskellite era came to an end.

There is truth in that interpretation of the recent past. Nevertheless, it remains a minor truth. As we begin to contemplate the recession of the Thatcher government into past history, even the disappearance of the Tebbits, Parkinsons and Ridleys from the political stage, and the ever-more emphatic emergence of a public agenda for the 1990s to which Thatcher's homespun but now distinctly threadbare philosophy relates most implausibly, we cannot but recognize that we are now at a hinge of vastly greater significance. The ending of the Iron Curtain and the Berlin Wall, of communist governments west of the Soviet Union, of a divided Germany, means the ending of the whole shape of Europe as we have known it for nearly fifty years. To a very real extent, it may mean the ending of a certain, dualist shape of the world. A communist Czechoslovakia was not just of European significance; its effect was far wider than that and more ambiguous. Thus the African liberation struggles from the 1960s to the 1980s in southern Africa could never have taken the course they did without a great deal of Eastern European assistance. Dualism in world power was of assistance to the underdog. Again, the effect of the Gulf War is likely to be no less great, though at present we cannot even begin to evaluate its full significance. Yet, in this very escape from predictability, the developments in the Middle East may not be so different from those in Eastern Europe. Here too, with every month that passes, from Lithuania to Romania, from the Ukraine to Yugoslavia, what must most strike one is the feeling that we are moving very fast into an era whose character is likely to be deeply different, but anything except clear, in its shape. All we can say with some confidence is that an age whose parameters were rather clearly defined in the 1940s is now over, and a new age is beginning.

SECULAR HISTORY AND RELIGIOUS HISTORY

Ecclesiastically, it is at least convenient that we have a change of face or label to accompany this hinge moment. At the end of January 1991 Robert Runcie retired as Archbishop of Canterbury after nearly eleven years of primacy to be succeeded by George Carey. Runcie was invited to become Archbishop by Mrs Thatcher just two months after she became Prime Minister. He leaves office two months after her. They were both Oxford undergraduates of the war years, suitably symbolic figures to preside over the final decade of the post Second World War age. They are replaced by Carey and Major, both Londoners from impoverished backgrounds who grew up in the 1950s and 1960s and who didn't go to either Oxford or Cambridge. In each there appears a quality of novelty, unpredictability, of lack of constraint by the past which makes them oddly suitable symbols for the moment in which we are. That can, of course, in regard to the individuals concerned, be a matter of symbol without substance. Major may prove just a boring replica of Thatcherite themes with a less strident voice, Carey may prove as much as Runcie a centrist presider over a Church he can hardly lead without dismembering, yet with a less sure touch. That does not much matter. It is the symbol not the substance of these men that concerns us at this point. The substantial unpredictability of the 1990s lies in the state of Eastern Europe and of Europe as a whole in response to the reintegration of its eastern half, of the Soviet Union, of the Middle East, of Africa, of the world environment, and – for us – the interaction of all these things with our own British society. In comparison with all this, the hinge quality of 1979, when the Conservative Party under Thatcher came to power, is rather small. And it will make still less difference whoever should win the next election, any more than it would be a matter of great moment to British society or the world if the Conservative Party were to capture the local government of the city of Leeds.

I have been speaking mostly about secular history. How far is all of this applicable to the religious history of Britain? At times, ecclesiastical history appears to go forward almost regardless of the world around it. All too many histories of the Church have been inclined to give that impression. But in reality it cannot be so. For better or worse, the world sets the Church's agenda, and in so far as the Church ignores that fact, it must become irrelevant and marginal. The more it reflects, grapples with, is wounded by, contests the central movements of secular history, the more it is cherished, hated, alive, true to its calling. That does not mean marrying the spirit of every age; it does mean being affected by it and by the needs of every age. An incarnational religion cannot avoid such involvement, and in point of fact the diversity and changeableness that are such characteristics of Christian history are the best proof that it is so. Nevertheless, the Church as a complex society with its own rules, leadership and specific internal problems inevitably also creates a trajectory of its own that may at times seem, even actually be, largely unrelated to the trajectory of the wider society. In so far as the two fall apart, the health and functionality of the Church must be questioned. But the two cannot all the same be identical. It would be unreasonable to deny the Church any right to have a history and problems of its own. Rather must a subtle balance be continually maintained between a certain appropriate in-history and one's concern for it, on the one hand, and participation in the challenges, social reversals, fresh insights of the community as a whole upon the other.

I suspect that our 1900 stargazer, if he had turned his mind to the churches, might not have been far out in his prognostications for 1930. The fact is that the ecclesiastical shape of things changed rather little in those thirty years. But his 1930 successor would have been far less likely to predict the 1960 picture at all satisfactorily; the immense advance of the ecumenical movement, the decline of the Free Churches, the growth, vitality and reform of the

Catholic Church, the huge change in what we may term the Roman Catholic theological mind, and so forth. Would the 1960s futurologist have guessed our present predicament? The failure of almost all specific ecumenical reunion plans and the reversal of a good deal of what Vatican II stood for, and yet at the same time the continued *de facto* merging of all denominational traditions within a Christian community that shops around and takes clerical pretensions and ecclesiastical frontiers increasingly lightly. Would he or she have expected the tensions over feminist theology or the upsurge of a new wave of Anglican clerical conversions to Rome, but, at the same time, a numerically far larger but less well publicized wave of Roman Catholics entering the Church of England? Would he or she have guessed that the mood of Christianity might be so very hard to categorize as it now seems to be? That the churches would in a sense have tried every conceivable 'movement', gone through it, and now not be clear where to go and yet, perhaps, actually feel purified by this very state of ecclesiastical agnosticism? Perhaps somebody might have guessed that, after the partial euphoria of the 1960s, we might well be in for a good deal of trouble, but one can hardly doubt that all in all things have not gone for the churches the way that almost anyone hoped they would a generation ago. Yet we would also, in 1960, not have guessed how very considerably in these thirty years the dynamism within the Christian world would have moved into the southern hemisphere. We can overstate this in regard to the way things are now, but we can hardly overstate the contrast between the situation today and the still very one-way, north to south, sense of control, influence and deference that prevailed in 1960.

THE ROMAN CATHOLIC CHURCH AND THE REST

The central internal issue of British Christianity over the last forty years, as I see it, has been that of the relationship of Roman Catholicism to the rest. It is still the central issue today, and must partially remain so for quite some time to come. Previous to the 1950s the Catholic Church was left out of almost everything. It was its own desire. It seemed simply too different to be included and the British Christian community was quite big enough, and had enough to do, without it. For the first twenty years of the British Council of Churches (founded in 1942), there was no great sense that this mattered. With the Vatican Council there was a sea-change and relationships between Catholics and everyone else were suddenly recognized as absolutely central to the ecumenical agenda. This was helped by a realization of just how much the Catholic Church had been growing numerically in Britain over the previous half-century. A British Council of Churches without Catholic members came to seem odd, and even almost counter-productive. A new sense, both national and international, of a unity of the Christian community, including Catholic, Protestant and Orthodox, in regard to all that is most serious both of faith and mission, had steadily grown and is now less something to be sought for than something actually seen to exist. The dissolution of the old British Council of Churches and its replacement in 1990 by a new body, with a rather different constitution and wider membership, 'Churches Together', in which Catholics fully participate, is powerful recognition of this, and provides a more significant hinge date than the change of archbishop. Through Churches Together, will British Christians of all traditions from black churches to Ampleforth Abbey really work together at the great challenges that face our society in the coming decades? That is the question. The remarkable pastoral partnership of Derek Worlock and David Sheppard in Liverpool already over very many years provides something of a model to start from. The way Archbishop Runcie and Cardinal Hume went together to Downing Street to speak to the Prime Minister on the eve of the Gulf War is another.

The Second Vatican Council and its ongoing impetus has changed everyone, Catholic and non-Catholic alike, and there is just no way in which we can go back to a preconciliar relationship. Yet our present state of relationship is too contradictory. It makes no Christian sense for Worlock and Sheppard never to share the sacrament of unity, a sacrament that in traditional Catholic theology is most certainly meant not just to embellish formal institutional unity, but to nourish unity between well-intentioned believers in all its fullness: spiritual, pastoral, hierarchical. It is a nonsense that we are welcomed to share communion upon the one side and sharply forbidden to do so upon the other – contrary, in fact, even to the tentative guidance of Vatican II. It is now manifestly clear that Rome itself is pulling steadily back from all the more radical dimensions of the Council's teaching and stressing only its more conservative and confirmatory aspects. We are in consequence caught in a condition of almost impossible ambiguity. The Roman curia only wants Christian unity in terms of Vatican I and a fully ultramontane model of the Church. Christian unity on such terms is as impossible now as it ever was and it always will be. Impossible for the Orthodox; impossible for Anglicans and Protestants, but most thinking Catholics do not want it like that either. John Paul II today is much in the situation of Gorbachev: glasnost has been offered, but when it became clear that it could only lead to the dissolution of a monarchical and centralized form of bureaucratic government and its replacement by the recovery of a free communion of churches, the offer of glasnost was withdrawn to be replaced by the repression of the Church as a whole – no less. Rome has not got thinking Catholics on its side anywhere in the world any more than the conservative forces in the Kremlin had the support of Lithuanians, Russians, Ukrainians or Georgians.

The Roman Catholic Church in this country is, in consequence of these contradictory requirements, at present, alas, a somewhat dreary, rather painfully declining phenomenon in regard both to laity and clergy, frightened even to recognize and analyse its problems. Many of us who are determined to stay within the communion do so in a state of greater or lesser filial disobedience, retaining sacramental communion with the Pope, but hardly intellectual communion. Effectively this situation, which is to be found in many other countries too, is paralysing both the Catholic community and the wider ecumenical community which can now go ahead neither with nor without the authentic co-operation of Catholics. It will certainly do much to make the Decade of Evangelism into a damp squib.

There is, of course, an element of over-simplification in this judgement. Some problems are being faced vigorously enough. Much of that vigour takes neo-traditionalist forms involving the reimposition of a basically pre-Vatican II model of doctrine, devotion and organization. I leave these out because they constitute an exacerbation of the very problem we are discussing. But there are other ways too. As the number of priests declines, so do the laity take over more and more of their ministry. At long last communion in both kinds has become an almost normal Catholic parish phenomenon and that means a large multiplication of lay eucharistic ministers. It is now normal to receive communion at the hands of a woman – something hardly conceivable twenty years ago. Last Sunday at an ordinary Mass, in a very non-elitist parish in the north of England, I received both bread and cup at the hands of black women: that might prove a strikingly symbolic prophecy. Only it seems in the archdiocese of Liverpool has there been a systematic and highly successful development of a married diaconate on a considerable scale. The wife of a Catholic deacon in Liverpool is now an accepted part of church life – and that may be halfway to the wife of the Catholic priest. So some things are moving, but the point of referring to all this here is that, while exceptional, it still indicates the only viable way in which the Catholic Church can move: into new forms of lay, married and female ministry, most of them long familiar in every Protestant Church. Their extension would not signify the simple Protestantization of the Catholic Church, simply because, while immensely liberating, they are not in reality alien to Catholic tradition. While a rather passive church-going will further decline, the range of ministries of the personally committed will greatly multiply.

How far can the Catholic community advance in directions in which Rome does not wish it to go? Almost certainly not far enough if the bishops do not stand together, not only within one country but between countries, to resist the imperialism of Rome publicly and even rudely. What the Catholic community of the diocese of Chur in Switzerland has been doing of late, the Catholic Church across Europe and the world must do: say 'No' to the Pope, just as the Lithuanians and Latvians have said their 'No' to Gorbachev. Failure to do so will be increasingly devastating not only for Catholics, but for the whole Christian cause, because all other Churches need the alliance of their largest and most powerful brother just as much as they are needed by it.

Britain is still today, as it has long been, one of the most important places in the world for the shaping of the ecumenical future – and particularly Catholic–Protestant relations. In this we owe a lot to Anglicanism. The Catholic Church in this country has seldom been seen as a particularly progressive Church and, in regard to the general tone of its clergy in the age of Hinsley, Godfrey and Heenan, that was undoubtedly correct. And yet, in reality, it too has been one of the greatest of bridge Churches: the Church of Newman, the Church of von Hügel, of Chesterton, of Christopher Dawson, Barbara Ward, Christopher Butler. The intellectual contribution English Catholicism has made to world Catholicism, American Catholicism especially, has been vast – out of all proportion to its numerical size. It has, of course, done it by mediating the scholarship, insights, and spiritual diversity of Anglicanism and British Protestantism. At the same time, no other Church has been more open to Roman Catholic influence than the Church of England. The life and theology of Anglicanism, in the twentieth century especially, is unimaginable without it. I do not mean the influence of early Catholicism or the Middle Ages, but of current Catholicism, of the liturgical movement, the priest worker movement, liberation theology, Lambert Beauduin, Etienne Gilson, Jacques Maritain, Pierre Teilhard de Chardin, Karl Rahner, Yves Congar, Hans Küng. One could go on and on. Behind everyone else the venerable Newman remains a shared legacy of an exceptional kind, almost a shared sacrament. It is this cross-fertilization that has got to go on in Britain for the sake of the Church universal and it won't happen if British Catholicism is increasingly maimed. Intellectually that is still not the case, but that is largely because British Catholic intellectual life has moved into universities where it is free from Church control. While not at present divorced from the institutional Church, it could become so.

The future here is still very open. The vigour of British Christianity as a whole in tackling almost everything else hugely depends, it seems to me, upon both the vigour of its Catholic section and the confidence and openness linking Catholics with the rest and at no superficial level. These things are today very gravely imperilled by the Vatican's neo-conservatism, but they are not, as yet, lost. They are not, however, likely to survive very much longer without a leadership on the Catholic side more militantly determined not to succumb to Roman pressure, even if that involves public confrontation. If that leadership cannot be episcopal, then it will have to be non-episcopal – as, in reality, has largely been the case in the past. If Catholics cannot resist re-Romanization in the ultramontane sense, then the rest must go on without them (just as the Canberra World Council of Churches meeting in February seems almost to have washed its hands of Rome and to be almost ignored by Rome – we are nearly back at Evanston). But make no mistake, the loss will be vast. The reshaping of the British Council of Churches was formal recognition of that. It is hard to be optimistic about the Catholic Church in the coming years, but unless one can be a little optimistic, one can only be deeply pessimistic about the general vitality and effectiveness of British Christianity as a whole over the next generation.

THE KEY ISSUES

Alas, I have become seemingly engrossed in the Church's in-history once more. What has all this to do with the great secular hinge we are now experiencing, with grappling with the agenda of the 1990s and beyond? Awfully little, and yet, I am afraid, a very great deal. Basically it has almost nothing to do with the principal issues of today's secular world; it is, rather, a carry-over from the Church's chronic inability to deal sensibly with its agenda in past ages, most recently that of the 1960s. It remains constipated from the menu of the past. Yet, until it clears its constipation, it cannot make use of its own resources to focus effectively on tomorrow's world, so I have felt forced to this melancholy review of that which currently within the Church's structures and internal life most impedes its mission.

What should it be focusing on? What will the issues be that require most effort and according to which British Christianity should be most exactingly judged as we move into the third millennium? Ever greater participation in a united Europe is the first and most obvious. A new relationship with Islam is the second and most spiritually difficult. Trying to assist Africa – at once the most growing sector of the world Church and the most catastrophically disastrous part of world society – is the third and most materially demanding. The environment is the fourth, but the one about which secular society thinks so much already and for which there are so many lively pressure groups at work that it is the one I need to speak about least. The fifth and last is the perennial theological task of intelligent believing beings caught between reason and eternity, but never a harder one than now, when we are confronted not only with the problematic consequences of an overwhelmingly powerful technology, but also with the understandable resurgence of very simple fundamentalisms – and, if we are not careful, the Decade of Evangelism may ensnare church authority to countenance the most simplistic of moral attitudes and the most irrational of religious claims.

Almost the final engagement of Runcie as Archbishop of Canterbury has been to confirm the Meissen Agreement between the Church of England and the Evangelical Churches of Germany in a service in Westminster Abbey. It is a good agreement and it goes some way to relate Christians in the two countries in the sort of integral manner that is now needed. But mentally to Europeanize British Christianity is a much larger matter than coming to agreements, and most certainly it is not a matter of relating just to Germany. Have we the cultural and linguistic openness and energy to grow genuinely European? That will be a hard enough task.

Relating to Islam will be still harder, but British Churches have a quite special responsibility in this regard. Islam is already an important British religion and it is going to grow in scale very considerably in the coming decades. It is also the religion of a profoundly alienated community. By 2020 Britain will be far more of an Islamic country than most of us can comfortably contemplate. At the same time, world Islam will be more active and expansive, maybe also more bruised, than ever. In several parts of the world there could be open Christian–Muslim conflict. If the coming decades have a quite particular character in church history, it may be because for the first time in centuries the relationship with Islam becomes the primary and dominating issue. Most Christians, even bishops and theologians, are woefully ignorant of Islam just as Muslims are mostly woefully unprepared for participation in the modern pluralist world, let alone religious dialogue. It requires enormous effort to produce quite small results on this front, but no front is likely to be more important, and probably nowhere else can Christians actually contribute more through a sympathetic understanding to the needs of society as a whole.

The intellectual issues of faith and theology are in no way new, and British Christianity has contributed more for centuries in this area than most, but equally they are not going away. There is a desperate need for genuinely theological thinking, relevant to an intensely secularized world of thought and a very pluralist society. There is not too much of that in the Church today. Now in all these three fields of European relationships, Islam and theology in general, the departments of theology and religious studies in British universities have a leading responsibility. We are, I believe, fortunate to have so many, and mostly so well integrated into wider faculties of large, neutral universities. In few countries, if any, is the position so good. We have links, actual or possible, with every other subject. We have no denominational control, but adequately open Church connections. Yet we have thought, it seems to me, far too little hitherto both about the strengths of our academic position and about the public, social role of departments of our sort in regard both to the Churches and to the world at large. We are underused (though not under-worked!). We have, I believe, a potential freedom for leadership in vital areas that Church hierarchies, and even ecumenical conferences and secretariats, most often do not and cannot possess. The future of the Church in this country, the future of our relationships with Europe, of the meeting of Christianity and Islam, of the viability of a reasonable faith, may depend enormously upon the university departments. The next thirty years will, I hope, see them taking a higher profile than hitherto, and a diversified but also more committed stance in relation to the world outside the portals of academe.

That leaves me with Africa. Probably it is the area to which least serious thought is still given, lowest in the list of priorities of governments, universities, the wise and the powerful. It is economically too valueless, too confused, too difficult to understand. Why bother? But it is likely to constitute the greatest, most difficult challenge to humanity over the next twenty years – a far, far greater challenge than we are yet aware of, ecological, social, political, medical – a challenge almost overwhelming in both its anguish and its apparent irresolvability. It is so much easier to persuade the

United States to spend billions of dollars dropping bombs on Iraq than to spend a tenth of that amount building peace in Africa. It is not a matter of annual appeals to save the victims of the latest drought or civil war, necessary as they are. It is an ongoing, constructive, multi-faceted response to a continent-wide crisis that is rapidly deteriorating. Of all outside countries, Britain has had, and still has, the strongest links with Africa and many of those links are Christian ones, relating to all the main Church traditions – Baptist, Methodist, United Reformed, Anglican, Roman Catholic. Much of Africa can fairly be called a Christian continent. It has more Anglican dioceses in it than any other. In Christian Aid, CAFOD, the CIIR and suchlike, we already have remarkable leadership in this field; indeed, in no other field has modern British Christianity probably been so effective. But that is still just a beginning. Here, as with Islam, it could with imagination come to function in a major bridging role, as interpreter, catalyst, continual lobbyist, determined not to allow the rich world to overlook its responsibility in justice for the poorest of continents.

British Christianity in 2020, as I hope to see it as I enter my nineties, will be a fellowship of Churches, as committed as ever to faithful prayer and rational thought, not too concerned about the details of institutional unity but happily conscious of a spiritual unity unirritated by canonical barriers, a fellowship deeply involved in ministries of reconciliation, between Christians and Muslims, between the West and Africa, between faith and secularity. It will be doing all this in the closest of communions with European partners from Moscow to Lisbon. If it can be even a little like that, I will heave one last sigh of relief and sing my Nunc Dimittis.

CHAPTER TWO

Growing Together

Anglican Identity and European Ecumenism

BARRY ROGERSON

The Past has revealed to me the structure of the future.
(PIERRE TEILHARD DE CHARDIN)

Teilhard de Chardin was talking about vast stretches of time, but what he said is just as applicable to this short-range forecast about the shape and future of Christianity in Britain some thirty years hence. We will need to discover the points of growth in the immediate past and the present that will determine the pattern of Church life in the year 2020.

There are several saplings that give us cause both for concern and for hope. There may well be others, but it is on the following points of growth that we will concentrate. They are the points of growth that suggest the nature of the life of the local congregation in thirty years' time; the relationships between the historic European Churches and the Church of England and the consequent impact these will have on ecumenical relations in Britain; and the relationship between Christianity and the other world religions, of which Islam is likely to be the most influential.

THE LOCAL CONGREGATION

Those who can remember the Church of England as it was in 1960 will reflect that there was a common Book of Prayer, so that you could go into any church and expect to know the service and the hymns; there was a ministry of the Church that was limited to the parson who was male, the lay reader, and maybe the Sunday school superintendent and teachers; the central government of the Church was still in the hands of the bishops, clergy and some laypersons and, while there were suffragan bishops, dioceses were very much in the hands of the diocesan bishop.

The services next Sunday will be ...

There is no longer a form of common prayer in the Church of England. Since 1965 we have gone through a major liturgical revolution in which the Alternative Service Book has helped to make the Eucharist even more central to the worshipping life of most congregations. The newcomer to the liturgical menu has been the ubiquitous Family Service, which has a non-liturgical form and makes its appeal to a wide age range of worshippers. With the introduction of numerous versions of the Bible, new hymn books and choruses, we have, to put it bluntly, liturgical anarchy, or a liturgical supermarket.

There have been some important gains. The central place of the Eucharist and the liturgical renewal that has taken place in all the mainline Churches has meant that there is now a clear family likeness to the Lord's Supper in all the Churches. This has important implications for the ecumenical movement, as we shall see later. If we have all discovered the place of sacramental services in the life of our Churches there have been significant losses as well. The Parish or Family Communion, which was meant to gather the whole Christian community together, has effectively drawn a tight circle round the local congregation, so that the casual visitor, the half-believer and the wistful seeker after faith now look in from the outside.

Unlike the well-grown Eucharistic tree, the Family Service makes it easy for the fringe Christian to join in. New Christians have been fed with simple preaching. Through the introduction of modern hymns and choruses there has been greater congregational participation in the worship of the Church. This new sapling will grow and threaten the

31

central place of the Eucharist as the normal Sunday morn-
ing service. While some will feel that this is a great loss,
others will be attracted by a more careful and reverent
approach to the common Christian meal, in which Christians are incorporated into Christ, and the promises of God
given to them at their baptism are renewed. The notice
board of the parish church in 2020 will have changed its
menu of services.

Once there were just vicars!

'All are called', a report of the Board of Education of the
General Synod said of baptized Christians, 'We are called,
for all of our days, to strive for a special quality of living. . . .
We all have gifts to be developed and used in God's service.
. . . And for all this, we have been promised God's grace and
spiritual strength.'[1] In most parishes there are laymen and
laywomen who play a part in the Sunday services. They
read the lessons, lead the intercessions, teach and preach,
and assist at the administration of the bread and wine at the
Eucharist. Their service is not limited to what happens in
church. They lead house groups, take responsibility for
pastoral care of the bereaved, the sick and the housebound,
and regularly prepare parents for the baptism of their
children and couples for marriage. Thirty years ago all this
was the prerogative of the local vicar. He had a small parish
and the time to perform every parochial task himself.

The sapling of lay ministry is thriving and will continue
to grow so that the gathering of all the ministries of the
Church into the hands of the priest will be drastically
reversed. Already significant questions are being asked –
'Why cannot a layman or laywoman be the minister of
baptism and the Eucharist?' The vicar of the year 2020 will
lead a congregation in which the ministry will be more akin
to that described in the New Testament, 'And his gifts were
that some should be apostles, some prophets, some evangelists, some pastors and teachers, to equip the saints for
the work of ministry, for building up the body of Christ.'[2]

Recently, clergy have looked to their peers for support and help to complement their ministry. This expectation has given rise to team and group ministries. The team has been the ordained ministers, though sometimes the team has included leading laymen and laywomen, though the inclusion of the latter has been infrequent. The received wisdom is that Christian ministers ought to be able to work together in teams. In fact, very few have been able to work effectively in this way. They have expended much time and effort in maintaining team relationships, time and effort that could have been used more effectively in the mission of the Church.

The team-ministry movement is not misguided, but it has looked in the wrong direction and forgotten, or perhaps misunderstood, the nature of the Christian community. The model of the Good Shepherd for the priest is a good one. Every congregation, and maybe every parish, needs a focal person, whom they can call their own. This is something we shall come back to when we look at episcopal oversight. This focal person does not have to do and be everything to and for that congregation, but there must be no doubt about who that person is. Teams and group ministries have fudged that relationship.

The future lies in a different direction. We have already seen the growth of shared ministry within congregations. The parish priest will not look outwards to a team of ordained clergy, but inwards to a partnership with the members of the local congregation. This change will be supported by the development of a system of review and appraisal among the clergy. Appraisal can benefit not only the minister, but also his family and parish. Appraisal can be hierarchical, in which case the minister deals with the archdeacon or the bishop; or it can be with consultants who stand outside the line management of the diocese. This development is only in its infancy, but there are those who believe that review and appraisal needs to incorporate some laymen and laywomen and the minister. The church notice board in 2020 will still have the name of the vicar painted on it. The team, however, will be the congregation and the vicar together, and not other full-time stipendiary clergy.

While the functions of the ministry will be shared with the congregation, questions about who can be an ordained minister in the Church of England will be resolved. The last twenty years have been dominated by the debate about the role of women in the ministry. Women were ordained in 1987 as deacons. They now wear dog-collars, are addressed as 'The Reverend June Butterworth', are authorized to baptize, marry and bury. For all practical purposes the general public regards them as vicars and their ministry is accepted. The number of male clergy in full-time ministry in the Church of England will be reduced in the next decade. The general public has experienced the authenticity of the ministry of women deacons. There is a growing number of Christians who can no longer see why women should be excluded from the ministry of the Church. The arguments will go on. There will be women bishops, priests, and deacons.

Those who belong to the Free Churches will not be surprised at women being fully accepted into the ministry of the Church. They already have considerable experience of women in ministry. Nevertheless, they still experience those who say, 'Yes, we will have a woman as our minister, but we would prefer a man.' They still find it difficult to place women in key appointments. The Church of England should, because of the way it makes appointments, be able to ensure that women can be nominated as incumbents, and, where they have the gifts and experience, to posts of greater responsibility and leadership. The church notice board will read, 'Vicar – The Reverend June Butterworth, MA'!

Bishops and dioceses

Archbishop Robert Runcie said on one occasion in the General Synod that suffragan bishops were a pastoral problem and a theological anomaly. The Report of the Archbishops' Group on The Episcopate 1990[3] chaired by

Sheila Cameron, QC, maintains that the norm is mono-episcopacy – that is, one bishop for every diocese. The demands of congregations and our society, together with the inherited diocesan structure of the Church of England, make it necessary to have several models for episcopal oversight. The large dioceses of London, Oxford, Chelmsford, Lichfield, Manchester, Salisbury and Southwark have developed area bishops; for all practical purposes, the episcopal oversight exercised by such area bishops is that of a diocesan bishop. Many of the remaining dioceses have given a greater or lesser degree of autonomy to their suffragan bishops. The theology is difficult, for the most part still appealing to a model of the Good Shepherd, but trying to incorporate a justification for shared episcopacy based on an analogy with the nature of God as Trinity. In reality, the Church of England has taken a pragmatic approach to the increasing demands made on diocesan bishops and has found various ways in which these demands can be met.

The Church of England has two provinces: York which incorporates fourteen dioceses, and Canterbury which has thirty dioceses. The relationship between an archbishop and his diocesan bishops is thus unevenly balanced. There is a growing desire for greater collegiality among bishops. This will be difficult to achieve with a House of Bishops whose membership would be over a hundred. Two dioceses cover London, making the oversight of that city very difficult to develop and exercise. To round the problems off, there is the vexed question of ecumenical geography. This latter concerns the geographical nature of the ecclesiastical areas of jurisdiction that Roman Catholics, Methodists, Baptists and the United Reform Church oversee. There is little coincidence between them, and, while in the past this has not been important, in an age when local ecumenical co-operation is growing, it has strategic importance.

Anglican ecclesiastical structures are based on a medieval pattern, though modified by a growing population and the demographic changes that have taken place during the last century. Just as team ministries are under question, so I believe the pattern of episcopacy in the future will be questioned and simplified.

The principles upon which new structures of episcopal oversight might be created are:

1 one bishop to each diocese;
2 an archbishop relating to a small number of dioceses so that there can be an effective collegiality;
3 areas of dioceses, which should where possible coincide with the areas of oversight of the other mainline Churches.

On the basis of these principles, a picture could emerge of up to eighty dioceses, with four archbishops in four regions – of which Canterbury and York would continue to be Primates and Metropolitans.

The church notice board in 2020 will have a varied menu of services. The staff will consist of one priest, listed perhaps as 'The Reverend June Butterworth'. There could be the coat of arms of an unfamiliar diocese.

THE ECUMENICAL MOVEMENT

The church notice board has been the means of suggesting which saplings will come to maturity to shape and underpin the life and mission of the local congregation. There will also be more subtle changes, and these will be seen in the development of the relationships between the various mainline Churches.

It has been repeated time and time again, so that the saying has gained some authority, that 'The ecumenical movement has run out of steam', and 'A generation that was not involved in the Anglican–Methodist conversations, nor in the post-war years of the World Council of Churches has no time for unity schemes.' Here we discover our second group of saplings. There are signs that suggest considerable changes are beginning to take place on the ecumenical front. These will radically alter relationships between the Churches in England and significantly alter the Church of England's focus of attention away from the Anglican Communion to Europe.

The Meissen Agreement

In Westminster Abbey on 29 January 1991, a joint Declaration of the Meissen Agreement was publicly proclaimed in an act of worship that included the celebration of Holy Communion. The agreement was made between twenty-five territorial churches in Germany, which include Lutheran, Reformed and United churches, and the forty-four dioceses of the Church of England.[4]

The Declaration is very honest. Without passing judgement, it recognizes that our ministries are not yet interchangeable, and differences remain in the exercise of oversight. The Agreement states:

> We commit ourselves to share a common life and mission. We will take all possible steps to closer fellowship in as many areas of Christian life and witness as possible, so that all our members together may advance on the way to full, visible unity.[5]

The background to the Agreement is complex. Because of the Leuenberg Agreement, the Lutheran and Reformed (i.e. Calvinist) Churches in Europe share 'altar and pulpit fellowship'. In more familiar Anglican language, they are *in communion* with each other. In Germany this goes further, and the various regional Churches, although coming from different traditions, make up a single Church.

The Meissen Agreement talks of 'being present at' the celebrations of baptism, Eucharists and ordinations. This does not imply that the Church of England and the German Churches have reconciled their ministries. It does show that there already exists a degree of communion and agreement. The most interesting proposal is that forms of joint oversight be established. In practical terms, this

means that the Church of England and the German Protestant Churches will meet together in order to speak and act
on a wider stage than they would normally do.

A united Europe

One of the features of the ecumenical movement at the
present time is the way in which dialogues once approved
by the participating churches provide a starting point for
others. The Nordic and Baltic Churches are seeking to
build on what has been achieved through the Meissen
Agreement. Unlike the German Churches, the national
Churches of Scandinavia (including Iceland), Finland,
Latvia and Estonia are purely Lutheran. The history of
relations with the Anglican Church is complicated by the
role of bishops in our respective churches. Nevertheless,
the dialogue continues to be promising. The Moravian
Church and the French Lutheran and Reformed Churches
have all expressed interest in closer links with the Church
of England similar to the Meissen Agreement.

Here is a step-by-step approach in the search for unity,
an approach helped by the text of *Baptism, Eucharist and
Ministry*. This text was completed by the Faith and Order
Commission of the World Council of Churches at Lima in
January 1982. No-one at that time foresaw that this text
would be the most widely used ecumenical text in modern
times. Some 400,000 copies have been distributed. The text
has been translated into thirty-one languages. The World
Council of Churches has received 186 official responses.
The Episcopal Church in the United States stated: 'We
rejoice in the convergence of belief which this document
represents . . . we regard it as a major step . . . in the work of
healing and reconciliation.' This is but one of the tools that the
Churches now have at their disposal to enable the bilateral
dialogues to lead to real steps towards unity.

There is a real possibility that ecumenical relationships
between the European Churches will be radically changed
in the next thirty years. The scenario could go this way.

The commitment of the Church of England and the German Protestant Churches to share a common life and mission is the first step. The involvement of the Nordic and Baltic Churches will eventually enable a reconciliation of ministries. The changed relationships between Anglican and European Churches of the Reformation must influence relationships with Churches of the Reformed Tradition in Britain. The saplings of Meissen and the talks with the Nordic and Baltic Churches will take us on a step-by-step journey towards the visible unity. There will, in other words, be a single market for the Churches of the Reformation in Europe. It is not easy to see the Orthodox and Roman Catholic Churches in this scenario. The time-scale for any significant change is likely to be longer than thirty years. Nevertheless, the ecumenical scene in Britain will be significantly changed. The co-operation between the main-line Churches will develop. This co-operation will be felt in a common use of church buildings and a further development of a co-operative pattern of ministry exercised by ministers of all the Churches. There will be more effective partnerships in community service and evangelism. By 2020 new ecumenical relationships will have a firm hold on the institutional life of the Church.

A change of focus

There will of course be losses, and it is likely that these will be felt in the way in which the World Communions are held together. There are signs that while the provinces of the Anglican Communion remain 'in communion' with one another, the pattern of close ties is changing. Once we could depend upon a common Book of Prayer. Once we could depend on a common culture that created and sustained the ethos of the Anglican Communion. Now we have liturgies that have a family likeness, but no common prayer. There is a continuing commitment to the Lambeth–Chicago Quadrilateral which forms the basis of a common belief which contains a commitment to the Scriptures, the creeds, the two sacraments of baptism and the Supper of the Lord and the Historic Episcopate. The latter has the important words, 'locally adapted in the methods of its administration to the varying needs of the nations and peoples called of God into the Unity of His Church'.

In Anglican ecclesiology there is provincial autonomy, while being in communion with the Archbishop of Canterbury. This autonomy allows every Province the freedom to develop patterns of church life that are appropriate to the history and culture of the society in which the Church is set.

Up to the present, much of the indigenous ministry of many Anglican Provinces has been trained in England, Australia, New Zealand or the United States. As such, the inherited European patterns of doing theology, developing spirituality and constructing liturgy had a common base. The next generation of Church leaders in Africa and Asia are likely to have had their training in places other than Britain. African and Asian Churches have discovered the connection between Christ and their own cultures.

The Church of the next century will show all the signs of regional family likeness and a rich diversity characterizing the regions of the world. The World Communions will have increasing difficulty in holding their member Churches together in an inherited coherence. In other words, the gains on the ecumenical front in Europe will be at the expense of the coherence of the World Communions. While this may not be a major problem for the Roman Catholic Church, given its ecclesiology, it will not wholly escape the pressures from local churches to develop their own life and mission.

If the Churches develop regional autonomy in their life and ecumenical relationships, then there will need to be an enhanced role for the World Council of Churches. Because it is a Council of Churches, and not a gathering of denominations, this will provide an arena in which Christians can share their insights, their patterns of worship and ministry.

In this arena, the universal character of the Church can be enhanced and maintained.

THE WIDER ECUMENICAL MOVEMENT

In 1945 London was still the metropolis of a vast empire that contained nearly all the Hindus, all the Sikhs, a vast proportion of Muslims, and enormous numbers of Buddhists. Yet it was unlikely that anyone in London would have known or talked with any member of a world faith other than Jews, unless they had been a missionary or a colonial official. Today, Muslims, Hindus, Sikhs and Buddhists are our next-door neighbours. Their children go to the same schools as our children. Their parents are part of the commercial, educational and political life of Britain. Their languages, cultures and religious faiths are practised alongside that of British and Afro-Caribbean Christians.

In January 1986, Pope John Paul II closed the Week of Prayer for Christian Unity with a homily in which he said:

> I launch a pressing appeal to all Christian brothers and sisters and to all persons of good will to join together during this year in incessant and fervent prayer to implore from God the great gift of peace. ... I wish to announce on this solemn occasion that I am initiating opportune consultations with the leaders, not only of the various Christian Churches and communions, but also of the other religions of the world to organise with them a special *meeting of prayer for peace*, in the city of Assisi.[6]

In Assisi on 27 October 1986, the Pope was joined by leaders and representatives of most the Christian Churches together with Jews, Buddhists, Hindus, Muslims, Jains, Sikhs, followers of Shinto, Zoroaster and the traditional religions of Africa and North America. They came together to pray for peace. This has parallels in Britain, but these gatherings have not happened without opposition. In December 1990, the Reverend Tony Higton took a petition containing 76,000 signatures to Buckingham Palace asking that the Commonwealth Day Service in Westminster Abbey be wholly Christian. This petition is but a symptom of the dis-ease that many Christians feel about the attitude they should take towards men and women of other faiths.

During the last few years, there have been muted but persistent objections to acts of worship in church schools that have not been wholly Christian in character, even though in some schools most of the children are adherents of other faiths.

This ambivalence is well illustrated by a resolution that came from the 1988 Lambeth Conference. It read:

> This Conference commends dialogue with people of other faiths as part of Christian discipleship and mission. ... Acknowledging that such dialogue, which is not a substitute for evangelism, may be a contribution in helping people of different faiths to make common cause in resolving issues of peace-making, social justice and religious liberty.[7]

The debate that took place around this resolution tried to find a way through the impasse that many bishops felt. The bishops who came from Africa and South East Asia, and lived in areas in which they faced a militant Islam, were concerned that dialogue meant a denial of the confession that 'Jesus Christ is Lord'. The British Council of Churches commended dialogue as a basis by which people of differing cultures and religions could live together in harmony. For many Christians this was a commitment to passive toleration only. Those who lived in the conurbations of the West Midlands and the North of England knew that passive tolerance is not enough. This lesson was brought home sharply to the world. Early in 1987, Pope John Paul II spoke about Fiji being a light to the world as far as race relations were concerned. However, by May of that year a *coup* had taken place that showed how paper-thin such relations had been. There had been separate development and a passive tolerance. Where racial tension is likely, coupled with the threat of violence, British community leaders know that there has to be an active tolerance based on friendship and understanding of one another.

To achieve this level of tolerance, the process of interfaith dialogue can help. There are four principles of dialogue:

1 Dialogue begins when people meet each other.
2 Dialogue depends on mutual understanding, mutual respect and mutual trust.
3 Dialogue makes it possible to share in service to the community.
4 Dialogue becomes the medium of authentic witness.[8]

When such a process has been entered into, Christians are forced to ask some very pertinent questions. For 2,000 years Christianity has been a missionary religion, and yet other world faiths are still very much in evidence. So, 'What is the place of world religions in the economy of God?' and, 'Is it necessary for everyone to be a Christian in order to be saved?' In other words, the Christian Churches have to ask themselves a series of questions about the place of Jesus of Nazareth in relation to men and women of other faiths.

When Salman Rushdie's *Satanic Verses* was published and the *fatwa* was pronounced on the author, white Europeans were surprised that such a medieval view could be taken. It became obvious from the many newspaper articles that very few Europeans understood Islam, even though there have been significant Muslim communities in most Western European countries for a century or more. The political upheavals in the Middle East have brought home the need to understand Islam if we are to live in peaceful coexistence. But to do that will require real dialogue, which most Christians would rather not face. Nevertheless, the questions have been asked and in the coming quarter of a century the Church must wrestle with them.

Some of the questions concern the Christian understanding of the nature and being of God, and not least the doctrine of the Trinity. In an interesting collection of essays and responses entitled *Christianity and the World Religions*, Hans Küng argues that it will not be good enough to repeat the old arguments. It is clear that Jesus of Nazareth pointed always to God's Kingdom, his name and will. God is one! He goes on in a barbed manner to say that Jesus would never have said, 'God is one nature in three persons and I am one person but in two natures.' Christians will be forced to ask themselves the pertinent question, 'How do we look on Jesus' relationship with God?'[9] The answer we give will determine the way in which we can relate not just to Islam but to Judaism as well.

The Church in Britain in 2020 will still be concerned about the relationship of Christianity to men and women of other world faiths. It may be that many Christians will still be content to live in a form of passive tolerance, but it is much more likely that there will have been an active dialogue between Christians and the adherents of other world religions. In Europe this dialogue will concentrate on Islam and Judaism, though not exclusively. The dialogue will, hopefully, make Christians more sensitive to what is believed and lived by those other religions of The Book.

CONCLUSION

There are many saplings around at the present time; some will grow to maturity and become significant trees in the life of the Church of England in 2020. The shape and life of the local congregation will have changed significantly, widening the number of Christians actively involved in the worship and mission of the Church of England. The relationships between the Churches, as they seek that unity which is both God's gift and his calling, will have dramatically altered the centre of gravity of the life of the Church of England towards the Churches of the Reformation and towards Europe. But the most significant challenge to all the Churches will be our relationships with men and women of other world faiths. It will be a time of theological ferment, in which the christological and trinitarian formulations will be under scrutiny. It will be a good time to be a Christian.

NOTES

1 *All are Called, Towards a Theology of the Laity.* London, CIO Publishing, 1985.
2 Eph. 4. 11f.
3 *Episcopal Ministry. The Report of the Archbishops' Group on the Episcopate 1990.* London, CIO Publishing, 1990.
4 *The Meissen Common Statement: On the Way to Visible Unity.* General Synod of the Church of England, 1990 (GS 931).
5 Ibid., p. 11.
6 *Assisi – World Day of Prayer for Peace.* Pontifical Commission 'Justitia et Pax', 1987, p. 13.
7 *The Truth Shall Set You Free – The Lambeth Conference 1988.* The Anglican Consultative Council, 1988, p. 218.
8 *Towards a Theology for Inter-Faith Dialogue.* London, CIO Publishing, 1984, p. 27.
9 H. Küng, *Christianity and the World Religions.* London, Collins, 1987, p. 116.

CHAPTER THREE

Sectarian Reactions

Pluralism and the Privatization of Religion

ANDREW WALKER

There is something deliciously decadent about futurology. It is delicious because it enables us to indulge our
fantasies, ride our hobby-horses, and say virtually anything we choose. It is decadent because such deliciousness
encourages self-indulgence at the expense of truth. This is
not only true for what passes as prophetic punditry: it is
true also for predictive social science. Social science has
not found a sufficiently rigorous methodology to control
the manifold variables of social behaviour, nor has it been
able to demonstrate that social prediction is even possible.

It is now old hat, but it is still true, that predictions that
are made in public run the risk that the public will either
falsify them or fulfil them. Marxist forecasts of the collapse of capitalism fall into this category: after all, both the
bourgeoisie and the proletariat have a vested interest in
the outcome of this prediction.

These preliminary remarks are a necessary caveat for an
essay of this kind because I want to make no claims that
anyone, least of all me, can make accurate guesses about
the future of British Christianity. Most social science
works with *ex post facto* analyses: with the benefit of (a) an
adequate explanatory theory, and (b) fairly clear data, we
can with some perspicacity and rigour discern the patterns
of religious life in the past. Max Weber's work on the
Protestant Ethic and capitalism would be paradigmatic of
this approach.[1] We might want to say that the work on the

development of sectarianism, such as early Methodism or classical Pentecostal movements, gives us a general picture of how sectarianism, under certain conditions, is likely to develop in the future.

We might even, when we are being religionists, change gear and move from descriptive social science to the prescriptive mode, and say that we can learn from the lessons of history. It is a feature, for example, of the so-called house-church movement that its members are aware of the mistakes of past sectarian history and are determined to avoid the fate of their precursors. (On the whole, it has to be said, they look like failing.)[2]

But even this sort of talk, while legitimate, is not without its problems. I agree with C.S. Lewis who believed that the only lesson of history is that there are no lessons of history.[3] Certainly we should avoid the often untested belief that the past is the known crucible for the knowable future. And the idea that we can at least talk of linear projections of present trends is comforting as long as one is convinced that history is linear.

I have my doubts whether such a conviction is founded on a solid basis. It belongs more to the ideological baggage of philosophical determinism, and its more congenial cousin probability theory, than to reality. Many future events have the strange habit of contradicting trends and projected forecasts. Who predicted, for example, when and that the Arabs would take over their own oil and change the face of Western capitalism? Who foresaw that Eastern Europe would collapse like a pack of cards?

And how many political commentators ever believed that Michael Foot would become the leader of the Labour Party or that Margaret Thatcher would become the longest serving Prime Minister of this century? Come to that, how many of us who are participant observers of contemporary religion had marked George Carey down on our cards as the man most likely to succeed Runcie as the Archbishop of Canterbury?

When it comes to pinpointing the accuracy of particular social, religious and political events, most pundits are as sophisticated and as reliable as the carpet bombing of American B-52s.

The future is an open texture of possibilities, both in terms of empirical history and what used to be called (until the post-structuralists deconstructed it) meta-history. Even those of us who still take eschatology seriously would be wiser in my opinion to see it as the fulfilment of creation rather than as the end of time. To take the latter view is to run the risk that we can plot the course, start the countdown, or at least read the timetable. On examination, searching for the keys to the future becomes not an exercise in history or theology, but a retreat into historicism and teleology. In this respect, many Christian futurologists are little different from Marxist sociologists.

Such a long prolegomenon is not intended to put a dampener on the proceedings so that I can say life is chaos and all we can offer in terms of forecasting is spitting in the wind. On the contrary, we can still offer educated guesses rather than silly ones, informed opinions rather than ignorant ones, rationally considered options rather than random skips of fantasy. This is less exacting than science and less compelling than oracles, but it is also less pretentious and more recognizably human. Indeed, in this book we have been asked to share our hopes with you as well as cast the runes. This, it seems to me, is still delicious but not decadent: for without hope there is no future worth predicting.

SECULARIZATION AND PLURALISM

Out of the many possible changes over the next thirty years, I have chosen to concentrate on what I would like to call the potential shape of Christian organization. In abstract, my thesis is that sectarianism will increase at the expense of traditional Christianity, though I believe that there will be a minority opinion, mainly of theologians and intellectuals, who will want to embrace religious pluralism not merely as a fact but as good in itself. My hope for the future is that British Christianity will avoid both options.

What kind of future Christianity will have in Britain is one thing, but it is important to begin with the prerequisite argument that religion itself will have a future. When sociology began in the nineteenth century with the positivism of Auguste Comte and the socialism of Karl Marx, evolutionary models were all the rage. For Comte, history passed through three stages, the theological or fictitious, the metaphysical or abstract, and the scientific or positive. The last stage, which Comte understood to be not so much the modern age but rather the final destination of human history, would witness the disappearance of religion as rational and scientific certainties dissolved metaphysical speculations into inalienable facts.

If Comte's positivism was unambiguously determinist, we find a more typical sociological response to religion in the work of Max Weber and Ernst Troeltsch. They were keenly aware of the disintegration of Christendom and the structural decline of Christianity in Europe. For them, the very processes of modernity – industrialization, bureaucratization, social mobility – undercut traditional authority, which was the hallmark of pre-capitalist culture. Religious authority, they believed, declined as it became urbanized and modernized, for modernization, in dissolving rural communities, also dissolved the sacred *Weltanschauung* that traditional communities upheld.

For many of the classical sociologists, it was not so much philosophical rationality or scientific thinking that they saw as the direct threat to religious authority (this was more the line that the logical positivists following Comte and Mach were to take). They saw the decline of religious authority as bound up with the functional rationality of modern living, where the eternal verities and numinous qualities of Judaic Christianity were repressed by the materiality and facticity of the scientific and technical culture.

49

Following Weber, Troeltsch, and to a lesser extent Durkheim and Marx, many religionists as well as some sociologists have tended, until recently, to buy into a secularization thesis that insisted that religion was in inexorable decline. Such a thesis has been particularly compelling in Britain. Church attendance has been continually dropping from the beginning of industrialization to the present time, so that today approximately only 10–12 per cent of the population regularly attend church.

As we enter the 1990s, however, we can see that such a frankly unsophisticated view – but still the popular one – of secularization is problematic. If, for example, it is the rational processes of capitalism or industrialization that has caused this decline in religion, why is it that in North America nearly half the population regularly attend church? Furthermore, there is recent empirical evidence that British church attendance is on the increase. Even the Church of England has shown a slight upturn on what had seemed to be its slippery spiral to extinction.[4] More noticeably, the Baptist Union and the evangelical and charismatic movements are experiencing substantial growth. This, as we shall see later, is a more significant indicator of future change than the unexpected blip on the downward graph of Anglican church attendance.

But in Britain since the Second World War we have seen home-grown religion augmented by the steady immigration of cultural groups who adhere to other world faiths. More recently, we have seen the import of numerous but small new religious movements. This has fuelled the phenomenon we usually call 'cultural pluralism', and in so doing has led to an increase of religious life in Britain.

Perhaps the most glaring weakness of the popular version of secularization, however, has been its over-concentration on institutional decline as measured by church membership. We need to remind ourselves that every survey on religious belief in Britain since the 1964 *New Society* report has shown that while 10 per cent or so of the population attend church, 75–90 per cent of the population insist that they believe in God.

Since the 1960s sociologists of religion have shown an increasing interest in what has variously been called 'invisible', 'latent' or 'incipient' religion. Canon Bailey's work, for example, demonstrates that while institutional Christianity is under threat, religiosity everywhere abounds.[5] People are incurably superstitious, and there is not only a fierce remnant of folk religion but also an increasing interest in the paranormal, the preternatural, and alternative belief systems.

On an impressionistic level, I have noticed over the last few years how students of religion are often indifferent to denominational Christianity and yet remain fascinated with religion. Spirituality is popular with many of them, but this is often divorced from the rigours of theology. They are interested in aesthetics and mysticism, but openly hostile to dogmatics. There seems little embarrassment when talking of wholeness or holistic approaches, but an acute unease when talking of holiness. Religiosity, then, is welcomed by them, but it is diffuse and freewheeling. It is perhaps closer to that pluralistic phenomenon some are calling the 'New Age'.

New Age is not yet a religious movement, in my opinion: it is a mood of resistance to modernity; it is a mutational reincarnation of the counter-culture of the 1960s – part of the Greening of the Age where spells, smells, and bells mingle in jolly confusion. Just as people are increasingly trying aromatherapy to complement their chiropractors, so crystals and mantras are augmenting traditional religious artefacts and prayers.

I think we can say categorically that it is mistaken and misleading to suggest religiosity will disappear or decline in the future: it may very well flourish. The question is, therefore, not will there be religion, but what sort of religion will there be? And of course an obvious short answer is that it will be diverse, syncretistic and volatile as one would expect in a culturally diverse society. Britain is part of the global village and can no longer be understood in isolation from or without reference to cultural trends worldwide.

But it is at this point that I want to interpolate that there have been aspects of secularization that will affect all future religion in Britain and particularly Christianity. This has been called by Dobbelaere, among others, 'laicization', and it is bound up with a structural understanding of pluralism and the privatization of religious life.[6]

Laicization, an untranslatable French neologism, denotes the fact that Christianity as the institutional Church of Europe has been swung by the processes of modernity away from the centre of social and cultural life and into its own privatized and peripheral sphere. Today in Britain Christian religion survives, like all other religions, as a leisure activity or as an ideological preference, but it has virtually no legitimate voice in the public market place. It has either been forced out, or it has voluntarily left the public arenas of government, education, welfare, and the scientific and technical bureaucracies.

Modernity is in fact typified by the fracture between its public and private life. This is one of the ways it is differentiated from earlier cultures, such as feudalism, where the split between public and private, especially at the face-to-face level of village life, was virtually non-existent. Laicization has helped facilitate the dichotomy of public and private in most Western cultures, leading to what is in effect a 'structural pluralism'.

We tend to think of pluralism these days either as a plurality of cultures and religions or, if we are theologians, we might be more familiar with, say, the theological plurality of a John Hick.[7] But it is structural pluralism that creates the institutional matrix in which cultural and theological pluralism flourishes.

And cultural and theological pluralism reside firmly in the private half of modernity's structural bifurcation. The private hemisphere is the world of family, leisure, sexuality, voluntary associations (including religion) and the personal search for meaning. The public hemisphere, to restate and expand what I said earlier, is the setting for the institutions of the modern state, professions, the shop-floor, and technological and scientific bureaucracies. What I have already called functional rationality, or what Buber would have called the I-It relation, characterizes life in the public arena. It is often experienced by modern citizens as objective, but impersonal and alienating, so that the private world becomes a sanctuary of withdrawal where the personal quest for meaning and relationship – the I-Thou of Buber – can be sought.[8] The privatized world of meaning – where religion has now made its home – tends towards more subjective and expressivist modes of discourse than the public world.

Because of the privatizing effects of structural pluralism, it is no longer accurate to call Britain a Christian nation if by that we mean a total culture – both public and private – that is nurtured and schooled by a Christian world-view. This is not to say that there was ever a time when Britain was deeply Christian. It is to say, however, that British society was permeated by Christian values and supported by Christian institutions that brooked no serious rivals.

Turning to cultural pluralism we can say that institutionally it is facilitated in the private world by modern urbanization, where social groups and individuals of all kinds live in proximity together but without the common rural ties of family, kinship, territory, and traditional religion.

Different social classes, interest groups and ethnic minorities jostle for attention and recognition in a world marked no longer by homogeneity, but heterogeneity; not cultural solidarity, but cultural diversity. Whether there is any longer an identifiable British culture is a moot point, but there are certainly many British subcultures. Mass media not only reflects this diversity, but helps foster it, so that even those still living in rural communities have access to and feel part of this cultural mélange. Indeed, the electronic media has the unique role in society of belonging to the public world, while promoting the cultural diversity of its private citizens.

It remains to be seen whether Christianity will ultimately embrace pluralism or seek to reject it, but it is important to realize that plurality, both structural and cultural, is the great social fact with which Christianity has to contend in the future. Indeed it is pluralism, in its richness, confusion, and diversity, that is shaping the future of Christianity in Britain.

WHAT WILL BE THE FUTURE SHAPE OF CHRISTIANITY IN BRITAIN?

In the light of this pluralism, I believe that sectarianism is the most likely development of Christian organization in the future. This, I concede, does not sound like good news; but wishful thinking is the parent of self-fulfilling prophecy and should play no part in forecasting, however inexact our efforts may be.

Sects have proliferated in the nineteenth and twentieth centuries as a response to the very processes of modernity that undermine institutional religion. Secularization does not cause modern sects, but its oppositional force to Christianity helps facilitate them as agents of religious resistance. Of course, as sects develop against the spirit of the age – or in order to rescue an apostate or lukewarm Christian tradition – they habitually splinter into new movements. This fragmentation then itself facilitates cultural pluralism, which continues to undermine the legitimacy and plausibility of Christianity in British society.

Nevertheless, although modern sects are initially unintended consequences of secularization that in turn become part of the problem of cultural pluralism, they do have admirable survival features. As resistance movements against the larger society, they seek to conserve their original vision against the encroachments of apostates and secularizers. Sects do not typically conform to the world: they seek to conform the world to themselves. In practice, this means the creation of a bulwark against plurality. This can either lead to an inward-looking preservation society in which others are excluded, or it can lead to an aggressive recruitment agency in which the sect competes with other cultural agencies for personnel. Christians usually call this evangelism.

Broad churchmen and women are usually resistant to the idea of the sect, thinking of it as odd, theologically deviant, or bigoted. But Weber's definition of a sect as 'the believer's church ... solely as a community of personal believers of the reborn, and only these' fits nascent Christianity very well.[9] And the great Puritan Congregationalist John Owen, in coining the phrase 'the gathered church', was enunciating the very voluntary principle that Weber and Troeltsch understood to be the essence of sectarianism.

It is true that sects have a bias towards triumphalism and exclusivism, but they are a successful recipe for survival in a situation of either persecution or adversity. The sect (unlike the broad Church, which Weber saw as 'a sort of trust foundation for supernatural ends, an institution necessarily including the just and the unjust'[10]) does not rely on natural community for its continued growth, nor does it overtly compromise with the secular forces of society: it creates community by association and, as I have already mentioned, forms an enclave of believers against the assault of alternative beliefs.

Structural and cultural pluralism will erode traditional Christianity at a faster rate than it will erode sectarianism, for pluralism undermines the cultural embeddedness of natural communities such as the parish, but is less successful against voluntary associations. Furthermore, the very openness of churches has already led them not only to embrace the secular world with increasing eagerness, but also to internalize its beliefs and methodologies. It is in Anglicanism, Methodism, the United Reform Church and increasingly in Catholicism that we have seen a succession of (usually liberal) philosophical and political fashions. This can be applauded or condemned on ideological grounds, but it is not unreasonable to assume that broadening out and embracing plurality will dissipate the distinctiveness of Christianity as a subculture and render it vulnerable to infiltration, take-over, or annihilation by its competitors. (In this respect, Islam would seem to have more nous than most of its rivals.)

Inward-looking sects, like diaspora churches, may be guilty of a siege mentality, but their very watchfulness and paranoia keeps them alive in a world hostile to absolute claims. But is this to be the future of Christianity? A head-down retreatist sort of religion where the gospel is divided into a thousand sectarian scraps, each snatch dimly echoing a distorted recording of the original but unfinished story?

Well, we must hope not, though *in extremis* such a situation would be better than no scraps at all, as we are reminded in Ray Bradbury's futuristic novel, *Fahrenheit 451*, where, in a world denied access to books, men and women literally become the chapters of classical and sacred texts by committing fragments of the literary tradition to memory. We should not be too sanguine about the unlikely possibility of this, for the thrust of MacIntyre's *After Virtue* and Bloom's *The Closing of the American Mind* is that the survival of objective truth in a pluralistic society is already in question.[11]

But over the next three decades we are not going to witness Christianity in a state of inertia or sectarian retreat: on the contrary, we are going to see sectarian expansion at the expense of the historic institutions. Or, to be more exact, historic institutions will also grow in so far as they choose to behave in a manner usually associated with evangelistic sects.

As we enter what Pope John Paul first called 'the Decade of Evangelization', despite the fact that many historic Churches have not the first idea of how to evangelize or whether they should in fact evangelize, there seems to be evidence of the beginnings of a British pragmatic 'have a go' mentality. It is not so much that there is a deep commitment to the *euangelion*, but the logic of evangelism, to borrow a phrase of Professor Abraham,[12] means for many Church leaders that most blessed of results: church growth (or, in the nomenclature of one member of the Church of England Board of Mission and Unity, 'bums on seats').

However, while Catholic and Anglican worthies are either dithering or genuinely doubting whether and how to expand, the charismatic Christians have already stolen a march on them.

Charismatics, and increasingly these days this tends to mean the majority of evangelicals, have remained faithful to a version of Christian orthodoxy while enthusiastically adopting the trappings of modernity. This has all the hallmarks of a winner, like the advert that proclaims 'a traditional service in the modern manner'. While in the last thirty years many intellectuals have moved from the death of God, through New Testament demythologizing and existentialist angst, on to either liberationist/feminist theology, theological pluralism, or post-modernist playfulness, charismatics have been attempting to drag alive and kicking what they think is the New Testament world-view – complete with miracles and demons – across the uncrossable ditch of the Enlightenment and re-present it in the streets of Leeds and London, where last year 250,000 of them waved their fist at the devil and shouted 'Make Way for King Jesus'.

Post-modernism may cut a dash at Clare College, Cambridge, but it does not cut much ice in the suburbs and inner cities of Britain where the Christian 'fellowships' of both the yuppies and the 'underclass' seem to prefer jollification to playfulness, supernatural power to difference, and gospel narrative to nihilism.[13] This is not intended as a cynical aside: it is my conviction that intellectual fashions – however profound – have little immediate effect on popular culture. And whatever else we may think about it, charismatic Christianity has chosen to do its evangelism in the streets and the market place rather than the rarefied atmosphere of the senior common room.

This, it seems to me, offers not only a lesson to liberal intellectuals, but also to conservative ones. The movement cloaked around Bishop Lesslie Newbigin known as 'Gospel and Culture', of which I am proud to be a part, is mistaken if it believes that it will significantly alter the culture's receptivity to historic Christianity by persuading more intellectuals to join its gang.

Charismatic Christianity is the fastest growing measurable phenomenon in the British religious scene, and I can see no evidence that it is about to slow down. It is also the most self-publicizing, and in many ways the most innovative.

Until the 1960s, this charismatic Christianity – which is the gentrified title of Pentecostalism – was thought by most sociologists to be a religion of the working classes. Pentecostalism, however, has shown itself capable of extraordinary mutation. Remaining phenomenologically much the same as it was when it began at the turn of the century – with its emphasis on speaking in tongues, prophecies, healings, and miracles – it has been grafted into the middle classes, becoming what might be called a sectarian implant in the heart of the historic Churches and forming a 'Church within a Church'. This neo-Pentecostalism usually advertises itself in the mainline denominations as 'The Renewal'.

Given this development we must not assume that we now have the measure of Pentecostalism, for charismatic religion is essentially adaptive. It takes root in alien soils and yet continues to plant out under its own banner, and not only with the fecundity of the older sects, but also as a new breed that has the hybrid characteristics of both sect and new religious movement. (The so-called 'faith movement' known colloquially as 'health and wealth' would be a successful example of this hybrid.)

But modern Pentecostalists have also adopted and adapted from American evangelicalism the methods of commerce and business in order to promote their message. While British charismatics do not yet have satellite TV, nor are they as wealthy as their American counterparts, they already major on high technology, build audio and video ministries around their many charismatic stars, create massive jamborees such as the Spring Harvest Festivals, and promote populism, as we have already seen, by calling out thousands of people to march on the streets. In 1991 and 1992 it is planned to extend the British marches into the cities of Europe.

Already there are signs that some of the self-styled 'new churches', such as the group known as the Restorationists, are following the American trend to create 'mega-churches' similar to the Church on the Rock in Dallas, Texas, or the Crystal Cathedral near Anaheim, California. While there is nothing yet to compare in size with these churches, which can boast some 5,000 members, the Abundant Life church in Bradford and Bracknell Baptist Church are examples of purpose-built buildings that cater for up to 1,000 regular worshippers. Under the direction of 'apostle' Terry Virgo, Clarendon Villas in Hove is a refurbished older church with a congregation in excess of 1,000 members.

When Pentecostalism began in the early 1900s it was a minority religion for the dispossessed. It has now come into its inheritance and, as it leaves the twentieth century, it is arguably the major religious force in Christianity for it has broken the boundaries of class, race, and nation in a way that few branches of Christianity have been able to achieve. As David Martin's acclaimed study of South American Pentecostalism has shown, it looks as if charismatic religion will be as significant in that continent as Methodism has been in ours.[14]

Religious revivals, as the Great Awakenings of America and early Methodism demonstrate, do not drop out of the sky: they are socially organized and all the signs are that British charismatics are organizing. They have come to dominate the burgeoning Evangelical Alliance and can put 80,000 people into the Spring Harvest residential holiday camps and call up 8,000 people to attend prayer meetings. At an international conference at Brighton in 1991, they were able to persuade the Archbishop of Canterbury to attend and the distinguished German theologian Jürgen Moltmann to address them.

Ideologically charismatic Christianity does not overtly capitulate either to secularism or to pluralism. It stands for the certainties of 'that old-time religion', and treats other religionists not as equals but as fair game in an open season of 'hunting, shooting, and fishing'. Some of the new churches consider the historic denominations to be moribund and invite people to leave and join them, or stay and renew their old churches according to the pattern of the new ones. And so the Church within the Church takes root again and the sectarian spores float across the formal boundaries of Church and sect.

Ironically, the charismatic sense of excitement, its preference for experience over doctrine, the tendency to value novelty against tradition, and its restless liturgy leave it open to the secular society it wishes to foreclose. More tellingly, its almost 'show-biz' obsession with the big-name charismatic stars, and its reliance on management and commercial techniques, renders it guilty of the old sectarian charge of worldliness. It preaches against the spirit of the age out of the spirit of the age. It stands up for orthodoxy, but in the rags of modernism.

CONCLUSION

I believe that Cardinal Suenens was right when he recently stated that Christianity can no longer rely on a benign culture to see it through.[15] It will make no significant contribution in the hurly burly of cultural pluralism without a distinctive voice and a dedicated discipleship. In this respect, I think that sectarianism in the voluntaristic sense in which Weber understood it is not to be violently condemned.[16]

I believe, though for the religious pluralist such a view is itself sectarian, that Christianity is not merely a good religion (actually it is often not that): it is the truest one. Not merely for me, or for my set, but for the whole world.

This also means that it is public truth, not my private opinion or some kind of permissible 'form of life'. It is not to be seen as an option, or a preference, part of the colourful tapestry of pluralistic Britain, or a playful pastiche of post-Enlightenment possibilities. It is the gospel of hope for a fallen culture.

But while I believe that there is nothing wrong with being tough minded, Christianity is not only about 'right belief': it is also about good practice. We need, therefore, to be tender-hearted. As Christians we are called to love our neighbours – indeed our enemies – and not to shoulder them aside.

Charismatic Christianity has a habit of being impatient with other expressions of Christianity. The new churches in particular seem to want to be part of the larger Christian body as long as they can lead that body by the nose. When one of the leaders of these churches can tell us that the new charismatic phalange will have to evangelize heathen Britain because no-one else is doing it, this seems to be not so much a question of myopia but a bid for power.

Indeed, my greatest fear for the future of British Christianity is that aggressive sectarianism of this kind will result not in evangelizing the secular society, but in inhibiting the ecumenical drive for the unity of the Church. Most of the spectacular growth of the charismatic new churches in the last ten years, for example, has been at the expense of other churches. Transfer growth is not, we must hope, what the Pope had in mind when he called for a Decade of Evangelism.

If Christianity cannot harness her impatient but powerful sectarian spirit for the good of the whole Church, then the unbridled sectarian spirit will do what unbridled sectarianism always does: break away from the common herd and run wild, taking fierce pride in having refused, unlike the other tame creatures, to be broken in by the forces of apostasy and establishment. And with the certainty that it is conserving or restoring the truth, the sect becomes the harbinger of schism and discerption.

There is an extreme irony here. Sectarian Christianity rejects cultural pluralism, in contradistinction to much liberal Christianity that embraces it either with joy or resignation. But the net result is the same: they both become swallowed up in the privatized world of structural pluralism where they participate in the babble of consumer religion where everyone shouts their wares but no-one knows how to conduct a common conversation.

It is this societal fracture, communal disorganization, and personal disintegration that are the very negative effects of the modernity which Christianity is called to redeem and heal. There can be no greater indictment of us if we remain simply part of the problem. It would seem, would it not, as if linear history, as we suspected, was wrong and circularity may be right, for with this scenario we are, existentially if not literally, back to the linguistic turpitude of the Tower of Babel.

If my analysis of British society in terms of structural and cultural pluralism is correct, the great challenge Christians have to face in the coming decades is to break down the Tower of Babel and reconcile the public and private split in our society. If the gospel is true and its light is not to be hidden, or apologized for, then it has to be not only proclaimed, but incarnated, into the structures of our culture. What sort of gospel is it that is received as good news by private individuals, but is prophetically irrelevant in economics, government or welfare?

Modern Christianity is still reeling from the mistakes of Erastianism and neo-Constantinianism. But the alternative to Constantine – and my hope for the future – is that British Christians will neither follow the liberal impulse and embrace pluralism as God's latest good gift, nor will they settle for aggressive and expansionist sectarianism at the expense of traditional Churches. We are going to need the commitment and voluntarism of sects in order to survive, but we must reject the smugness, impatience and exclusivity that are their usual corollaries.

What this will mean in practice is that we have to become missionaries to our own culture.[17] This is not an overnight affair. Like the Apologists of the second century, we will need to take on the conventional wisdom of the day and turn it inside out with the truth of the Christian faith. Missioners accept as axiomatic that their job will be a long haul. It takes time to change thought patterns, untested traditions and comfortable plausibility structures.

Christendom may be dead, but we who are its survivors dare not retreat behind the barricades of cultural isolation where we become merely one island of meaning in a vast but private sea where other islands float in splendid isolation. We are called to take the gospel to the whole culture, and that includes not only sailing to the other islands in the sea, but back to the mainland that we have left behind. We must return under the old banner of the cross, but this time we will not come to conquer but to sojourn.

NOTES

1 M. Weber, *The Protestant Ethic and the Spirit of Capitalism*. New York, Scribner, 1958.

2 A. Walker, *Restoring the Kingdom: The Christian Struggle for the Modern World*. London, Hodder & Stoughton, 1988, ch. 12.

3 C.S. Lewis, 'De Descriptione Temporum', in *Selected Literary Essays*. Cambridge, Cambridge University Press, 1969, p. 3.

4 There is a 1.5 per cent increase according to the *Church of England Yearbook*. London, 1991. The statistics do not make it clear, but it would seem likely that the major growth is at the charismatic/evangelical end of the Church. This is undoubtedly true of the growth within the Baptist Union.

5 E. Bailey, 'Religion of a Secular Society'. Unpublished Ph.D. thesis, University of Bristol, 1976.

6 K. Dobbelaere, 'Secularisation: A Multi-Dimensional Concept'. *Current Sociology*, 29/2, summer 1981.

7 J. Hick and P. Knitter eds, *The Myth of Christian Uniqueness*. Maryknoll, Orbis, 1987.

8 M. Buber, *I and Thou*, tr. R.G. Smith. Edinburgh, T. & T. Clark, 1959.

9 Quoted in M. Hill, *A Sociology of Religion*. London, Heinemann Educational Books, 1973, p. 47.

10 Ibid., p. 47.

11 A. MacIntyre, *After Virtue: A Study in Moral Theology*. London, Duckworth, 1981; A. Bloom, *The Closing of the American Mind*. New York, Simon & Schuster, 1987.

12 W. Abraham, *The Logic of Evangelism*. London, Hodder & Stoughton/C.S. Lewis Centre, 1989.

13 See D. Cupitt, *Creation out of Nothing*. London, SCM, 1990. Cf. M.C. Taylor, *Erring: A Postmodern A-Theology*. Chicago, Chicago University Press, 1987.

14 D. Martin, *Tongues of Fire. The Explosion of Protestantism in Latin America*. Massachusetts, Basil Blackwell, 1990.

15 L.J. Suenens, in A. Walker, ed., *Different Gospels: Christian Orthodoxy and Modern Theologies*. London, Hodder & Stoughton/C.S. Lewis Centre, 1988, p. 56.

16 In the case of many black Pentecostalist churches, it is their sectarian structures that have enabled them to resist the encroachments of the white society both religious and secular. See P. Mohabir, *Building Bridges*. London, Hodder & Stoughton, 1989.

17 This, it seems to me, is the unique contribution of Bishop Newbigin to the debate on gospel and culture. See L. Newbigin, *The Gospel in a Pluralist Society*. London, SPCK, 1989.

CHAPTER FOUR

People's Church

Christianity as a Movement of the Poor

JOHN J. VINCENT

1 THREE TYPES OF CHURCH AND CHRISTIANITY

I see the future of Christianity in Britain as being along three main lines, representing three different types of Church and teaching, and upholding three 'versions' of Christianity.

(i) The institutional Churches, representing chaplaincy Christianity

The first line is the continuation of a basically culture-affirming style of Church, in which Christianity functions as a chaplaincy service to the changing society, and in which Christianity contributes from time to time 'responsible comment' from within, on the basis of a still significant number of believers who see their Christianity as lived out essentially within the structures and institutions of society. The denominational base of this style of Christianity will continue to be predominantly Anglican, though most Roman Catholics and Free Church people have now been assimilated to this position. The theology can be sacramental, evangelical or broad Church: the result will be extremely similar. Christianity on this model is a leavening influence within society as a whole, pointing to and supporting the good in that society, but basically taking its tune from it.

(ii) Extra-denominational churches, representing conservative Christianity

The second line is the continually growing extra-denominational varieties of Christianity. The house churches and the black-led Pentecostal Churches were easily the most significant developments in Christianity in the 1970s and 1980s. The varieties will increase in the future, with the development of diverse forms, such as a Christianity of the New Right, varieties of New Age syncretistic Christianity, and new extra-denominational conservative churches. Christianity on this model is a leaven that works within the individual, securing salvation and holiness within the corrupt society, which despite its corruption, is still expected to behave morally.

(iii) People's Churches representing radical Christianity

Alongside these two, I envisage the development of small grassroots groups and congregations. The Para Church of the 1970s and the European Base Church Communities of the 1980s are small models of this development. It will be a development of the many groups and communities at present within and alongside the existing denominations, often existing as worship cells in urban areas led by ex-middle-class people, but discovering a new popular Christianity at the base of society, and joining with surviving or newly emerging churches of the poor within existing denominations. Christianity on this model is the leaven of small alternative communities, at work at the bottom of society, pioneering – and at times securing justice – for the poor.

Since the third is the most contentious of the three lines – and undoubtedly the one that will require most work – I concentrate my attention entirely upon it.

Behind the People's Church model, however, lies an even more significant theological model. It is that of Christianity as a Movement. Since a People's Church is needed only because Christianity as a Movement has to be serviced, I must immediately say something about that.

2 CHRISTIANITY AS A MOVEMENT

The concept of Christianity as a Movement stands in opposition to that of Christianity as a religion – the concept that basically informs the first two models of institutional Churches and extra-denominational churches. In both cases, Christianity functions as a religious element within the existing society, as 'the glue of society' (Tertullian), as the cohesive force or the compensating spiritual dimension – the emphases differ greatly.

Readers of the Old and New Testaments will be familiar with quite another tradition. Faith in the living God is neither the cohering, unifying factor in the midst of a society, nor the religious or spiritual dimension functioning within it or alongside it. Rather, faith is a constant call to a specific, often hard, alternative secular reality – a way or attitude or policy proclaimed as possible within history. This alternative way is the way of Jehovah, whose name is 'I will be what I will be', and of Jesus who points to the Kingdom and embodies its life but refuses to set it up as an institution. People are called to be followers or disciples of this Way of Jehovah or Way of Jesus. They become part of movements and groupings within history that run behind the living alternative possibility (Jehovah or Jesus).

The most significant discovery in theology in my lifetime has been, to me, the rediscovery of Jesus as a real person in history, and the reassertion of obedience to Jesus along the lines of the synoptic Gospels, as over against the Catholic and Protestant belief-systems along the lines of Paul. This now needs to be carried to its logical conclusion. We need a radical theology based on discipleship to Jesus, a new systematic based on faithful practice. We do not need creeds, but 'rules for the road', for those who wish to be disciples to the ongoing, emerging God, incarnate in the Christ today.

The tradition of Christianity as a Movement has its origins in the New Testament itself. A radical Christianity may there be traced, especially in the first three Gospels, which bear witness to the basic assertion of Jesus in proclaiming the Kingdom of God, and its consequences for followers.

The assertion of the Kingdom of God in the practice of Jesus has two immediate consequences.

First, a new situation is announced and at least in part embodied, which affects all social relations, and which especially brings those at the margins of society into the centre of interest, in terms of healing, reconciliation and reconstitution. The gospel is a movement of the common people. It is a movement that elevates the status of the poor, overturns the power structures of religion and state, and proleptically unleashes a force of humanization, secularization, egalitarianism, reversals and ecumenicity, into society and history.[1]

The second consequence of Jesus' assertion of the Kingdom is the creation of an alternative, disciplined group, based on those who 'give up all' to join the movement. Leaving behind previous commitments, they become a 'collegium', a working party, a revolutionary caucus, representative of the old holy people – hence the number of twelve disciples – but also representative of the new society itself in miniature. The model of this new community is found in the synoptic Gospels – especially, I believe, in Mark's Gospel.[2] The Gospel of Luke and the Acts of the Apostles indicate the strictly parallel nature of the post-Easter disciples' activity to that of the pre-Easter Jesus and disciples. Both reflect a committed communitarian movement in service among the poor.[3]

Thus, New Testament Christianity shows the elements of a popular, liberating style of Christianity geared to the socially and economically deprived, and manifesting itself immediately in a small group of people who became novices in the movement. The popular radical Christianity and the People's Church belong together.

The history of a people's Christianity in Britain remains to be written. The control of educated clergy and the dominance of certain classic but highly limited formulations of doctrine have combined at most times to distance the common people from presuming to have any claim to understand Christianity, much less to claim to be its logical or proper inheritors. What had been intended to be good news for the poor was invariably mediated downwards by the non-poor, in whose hands the whole enterprise naturally was transformed from the good news of present change to present continuance of oppression. The latter, of course, was good news for the non-poor, but not for the poor.

The elements of a grasp by the common people upon the heady prospects and promises of a Kingdom of God on earth, of God's will being done on earth as in heaven, can be traced through bits of English history. Chaucer, Piers Plowman, the Lollards, John Ball, the Levellers, the Diggers, the Quakers, the Commonwealth, John Wesley's Religious Societies, Evangelical City Missions, Primitive Methodists, Anglo-Catholic Religious Orders, all deserve to be assessed from this point of view. Each in varying degrees and in widely differing circumstances and styles were attempts to assert and embody a gospel-centred community of Christianity among the poor which fulfilled at least in part the promise of a Kingdom of God upon earth.[4] The strong wine of apocalyptic and millenarianism greatly influenced the earthly utopianism of this tradition.[5]

3 PEOPLE'S CHURCH

Likewise, we may trace in most of these manifestations of radical Christianity the style of church as 'popular' or 'of the poor', existing in small prophetic groupings, often persecuted, invariably condemned. The small communities of people committed to the new way, and embodying parts of it, always exist alongside the claims for a new society.

The 'People's Church' invariably has several levels. First, there is the prophetic or charismatic leader, either educated or uneducated, who frequently discerns the rise of a new consciousness or possibility among the oppressed, and gives voice to the new hopes. Second, there is the inner circle of collaborators, organizers and practical workers, who form the administrative and sustaining cadre, and who usually consist of some upper-class 'converts' plus some lower-class leaders. Third, there are the committed members and supporters, who give time and energy to the movement, and from whose ranks the second group can be selected. Fourth, there is the wider group of followers, or 'adherents', or 'hearers', who can be looked to for potential members of the third group. I believe that this model of 'levels' can be illustrated from the levels of discipleship in the Gospels.[6] It certainly is reflected in historical instances elsewhere of similar kinds of small Christian communities in specific neighbourhoods.[7]

I see the recent heritage of this 'People's Church' in Britain in the nineteenth-century People's Churches, the Co-op Guilds, the Labour Churches and the Adult Schools.[8] All of these flourished around the turn of the century. Even their replacements, the Gospel Halls on housing estates, enjoyed some of the characteristics, as did the mission halls and community centres of the denominations, during the inter-war years. The latter were unfortunately largely closed by the denominations that opened them, as they concentrated back on the middle-class Churches with which they felt more at home.[9]

Several 'Faith in the City'-type projects of the Church Urban Fund are very like People's Churches, and it remains to be seen how the whole Church of England will deal with them. Especially, some striking Christian communities in deprived areas, set up by the Anglican and Roman Catholic religious orders, belong to this genre, and seem to be able to deal with the reality of an extra-parochial, lay-led Church, which is not part of the central priest-led Mass of the parish. A few years ago, in 1987, the Methodist Conference called for 'House Congregations', but I did not hear of any on my journeyings around Britain as President of the Methodist Conference, 1989–90. We now have five shop-front churches, and rather more churches in houses, which are steps in the right direction. All these are hints, though only hints, of a People's Church.

The Base Ecclesial Communities of Latin America are obviously crucially important elements of contemporary inspiration in the People's Church Movement. However, it is a mistake to think that a People's Church in Britain could be modelled on them. Rather, it must adopt its own style, and become the Church of the dispossessed in Britain. I shall turn to a comparison of People's Church and Base Communities at the end of the chapter.

Congregations and groups that broadly come under the heading of 'Basic Christian Communities' in Britain during the last twenty years have been largely middle class. The concept of the grassroots Church has been with us since the 1960s. John Pairman Brown argued that Christian resistance needed 'A Liberated Zone', which might be an 'underground Church' where liberation could be pursued.[10] In the 1970s I used the term 'Para Church' or 'Alternative Church' to describe such extra-denominational congregations, and described the life of four such congregations in Britain,[11] three of which certainly continue to the present. Meantime, European 'Base Communities' have arisen, largely Roman Catholic in origin, but including others.[12] Meetings of such 'Base Christian Communities' take place regularly now. The Ashram Community, with which I have been associated since its inception in 1967, plainly belongs to this type, and Ian Fraser's latest book on the Iona Community places it there also.[13]

These largely middle-class European grassroots congregations are extremely significant, as I have asserted elsewhere. But churches of the common people in Britain are plainly something different, and it is with them that I am concerned here.

What, then, does a Church of the People, or Church at the bottom, look like? Let me describe two in Britain known to me.

4 TWO PEOPLE'S CHURCHES IN BRITAIN

The first People's Church is an ecumenical meeting of people from a deprived housing estate near Wolverhampton. A dozen people gather there on a Thursday evening. I was present on one occasion when it was clear that the dozen people from many cultures who were participants, were people previously all but entirely non-church.

The full story of Margaret Walsh and the Hope Community of the Society of the Infant Jesus is told in a recent publication, *Here's Hoping*.[14] The description of the Thursday evening 'Faith Alive' goes as follows:

'Faith Alive' is held on Thursday nights and begins, for those who want it, with Scripture, which is read and shared in the light of our experiences. Some are almost totally unfamiliar with the Gospel stories and are hearing the Word of God for the first time, like those who heard Jesus, and it is refreshing to experience their reactions. Our friends here are wonderfully open and free in their sharing; they are unafraid to express both positive and negative reactions, no matter what others might think or expect.

Scripture sharing is followed by small group work with everyone who comes, during which we share our values on a chosen theme. After this, there is an opportunity to hear about some new legislation or local initiative, which is likely to affect the estate, and we go on to discuss how we can respond to these developments. We also have a role for a foreign affairs correspondent, so that we can keep up to date on world affairs and perhaps see our own situation in a broader context. Matters related to the Third World and to situations of people which seem far worse than our own, always give rise to lively discussion and real concern for brothers and sisters in greater need. Although we have little to give materially, we have responded by writing and signing letters of encouragement and support to prisoners of conscience and we have been in touch with various banks regarding Third World debt, etc. It is a great shame that the people here have not got the means to lessen the gap between the 'haves' and the 'have nots', because they are so full of human goodness and compassion.

We believe in celebrating the joyful mysteries of life, so birthdays are remembered, new-born babies welcomed and cultural feasts are given due honour, usually with a multi-cultural mix, e.g. Irish coffee drunk to the beat of Reggae music. We also have regular 'shared tables'. Someone hosts the evening and we go along with food to share, and also with our Bible and hymn books. Many are slow to invite others into their homes because they may not be able to offer chairs to sit on or a cup of tea. Also, loneliness and isolation can leave people uninterested in caring for their homes. However, 'shared tables' can provide the necessary motivation for people to start home-making and offers others in the local community the chance to help them.

My second example is a small group of Christians on the Flower Estate in north-east Sheffield: the Upper Wincobank Undenominational Chapel. It is a beleaguered 150-year-old chapel set in the midst of a very deprived housing estate.

Every Sunday the service begins with twenty to thirty children, their teenage teachers, plus Gill and Susan. First, there is fifteen to twenty minutes of mildly charismatic songs, sung from locally duplicated sheets, accompanied by Susan's guitar. In between, children read prayers or Bible stories or contemporary tales, taken from popular glossy-back children's books. Then they say 'You can go now', and with this *missa est* the adult congregation of five to ten go into another room; or else the children themselves leave, now that we have a newly built upper schoolroom. Led by a Chapel member, or myself, the adult worship takes place. Here we sing hymns by request, read Scripture together, share notices and make quick decisions, mention any problems on the estate, at the Chapel, or among local people, and in the time remaining have a short, often participatory, 'sermon', usually a Bible Study related to local life and issues.

Planning is done at a Chapel meeting. There is no 'membership', as they believe that 'whoever comes is a member', so the meetings are open to all. Until August 1988 there were fifteen to twenty community workers from our Sheffield Churches Community Programme Agency, and weekly activities included the Rainbow Club (old people's Bingo), two lunch clubs for the elderly, a mothers' and toddlers' club, a 10–12s club, and an arts workshop. Now all have disappeared, though the Sunday School arranges camps, outings, and a weeknight club.

Services are chaotic, decisions are by consensus, strong views are expressed not expecting to be resolved, people do what they want to do. But it is a happy, open community. 'We're a funny lot here', they tell you. 'But we like it this way.'

Every few weeks, we discover newly stolen children's presents, or newly broken tiles, or faeces in the concert hall, or more dry rot, or some Trust refusing us money, or some official criticizing us, or some new scheme or project running aground. We get angry, and blame each other. But it does not last. 'Now it's something else', they say. 'Still, all the bother helps keep us together.'

5   SOME CHARACTERISTICS OF A PEOPLE'S CHURCH

Where the Church does exist in places like Heath Town or the Flower Estate, it has very clear characteristics. This does not vary with denomination. Some of the churches of this kind are not of mainline denominations, but there are Church of England and mainline denominational churches like this. I have worked with many ministers and members of such 'People's Churches' over the last twenty years through the Urban Theology Unit. My conclusions are that there are very distinctive characteristics of such churches. The portrait would go as follows:

1 The church life and worship are strongly idiosyncratic, and vary enormously from place to place and from group to group.

2 Strange, unusual and unorthodox habits are allowed, and given space, and have to be encouraged by everyone, especially anyone 'in charge'.

3 Strong local traditions about church membership often exist, concerning who can do things and who cannot.

4 Local leadership, being in it together, and loyalty to local traditions are more important than hierarchy, denomination and party-line.

5 Local leaders are often self-appointed and do their own thing, but others delight in this and connive at it.

6 Events are often spontaneous, quickly arranged, and chaotic.

7 There is nothing more important than the person. A crying child, or someone ill, or a mishap in the service totally dominates, and has to be attended to immediately, rather than hushed up or the person taken out.

8 Personal performance, even if appalling, inaudible, or incorrect, must always be encouraged and heard by the rest.

9 Children have a very special place, and anything they do is all right, not because it is good, but because they are doing it.

10 Speech between people is almost always stories, anecdotes, gossip concerning experiences and happenings. The person projects herself/himself through the story, and the story must not be denigrated.

11 Knowledge of and collaboration with other local groups is more important than to be an acknowledged part of any established power structures.

12 There is often a fierce isolationism, suspicion of 'incomers', dislike of outside professionals, and a tenacious loyalty to long-standing customs and relationships.

13 Dishonesty is not criminal. People are entitled to get whatever they can. 'If you don't look after yourself, no one else will.' 'If someone else is stupid enough to be

ripped off by you, it is their fault.' These are elements in a strong alternative popular morality.

14 Love for spouses, children and parents are prime virtues, and infinitely more important than any other loyalties. Lawbreakers who have these are OK. But people who break up marriages, put parents in homes, or kids onto the streets, are outcasts.

15 Outsiders are there to be used, especially social workers, ministers, etc. 'They come onto the estate to help us, and we welcome them. When they've gone, we ask each other what we've got out of them.'

16 People either 'fit' or they don't. People cannot 'earn their way in'. 'If your face fits, that's fine, it doesn't matter who you are. But if it doesn't fit, you'll always be an outsider.'

17 There is a strong but gentle expectation of incompetence and failure. 'It's a miracle if anything works here.' 'If you can get anything done at all, that's great – even if it's not great in itself.'

18 The key people around whom things happen are often not the 'leaders' in the area, but those who create the atmosphere, the earth, the womb, within which things happen. Activists often only exist because of such people at work within communities.

19 Women are frequently the key figures in the churches. They perform overt leadership roles. They outnumber the men, and are invariably stronger than the men. When a 'strong line' has to be taken, it is the women who will take it.

20 There are few men in the churches. Frequently, the men are less competent than the women, but the women like to have a man in the role of apparent leadership, even if he has to be prompted, supported and apologized for.

21 People visiting the church service from outside often feel it to be 'lacking in a sense of worship', 'crude' or 'chaotic'. The worship is in fact so 'indigenous' as to be fully intelligible only to the 'locals'.

22 If there are paid ministers, they are usually accepted

in the same way as other 'educated' people like teachers or social workers. They are not 'one of us', and usually do not stay long enough to be taken too seriously.

Such, then, are some of the characteristics of 'People's Churches' as they exist at present, within and alongside the denominations.

6 PEOPLE'S CHURCH IN THE FUTURE

I believe that a proper strategy for Christianity in Britain should include a patient working at the model of the People's Church.

It will not be easy.

But it is exactly what is needed in our present society – and in almost every part of Britain.

In the Urban Theology Unit, we work with clergy and ministers of all churches in what we have called the Urban Ministry Course. Most groups include several clearly intentional and well-motivated ministers, whose task is that laid upon them by their denominational employers – notably, that of maintaining an existing church building with its existing church membership, and seeking if possible from that base to care for the pockets of deprived or lower-class people who dwell in sections of their parishes or areas.

Typically, in Anglican terms, a vicar is responsible for a geographical parish, which would be provided with a church building in the older or more central or more prosperous part of his parish. At the other end of the parish, or in some less accessible section of it, there is a council housing estate, or an area of industrial housing, which comprises the 'urban priority area' of the parish. The vicar, and to some extent the parish, feels a sense of responsibility for the needy area. So they appoint a Church Army officer, or a deacon, or a parish worker, or a community worker, to work in the needy area, with the hope that people can be brought together from the area who would attend the central parish church. A first step might be the setting up of house groups in the area, even the

holding of kitchen Eucharists, as Ernest Southcott pio-
neered in Halton, in Leeds, in the 1950s and 1960s. Or lifts
are arranged, and even mini-buses laid on, to bring the
people into the central church, 'so that they feel part of the
whole Church family'.

The philosophy of *Faith in the City* and the Church
Urban Fund is different. It is to create and support the
Church among the poor; among the 99.2 per cent of people
the Report says are largely outside the present Church of
England. But the base for this is still usually the local parish
church, clergy and members, and it remains to be seen what
the long-term result of Church Urban Fund projects will
be.

Similar stories could be told from other denominations. I
tell the Anglican one only because it is likely to be most
widely recognized.

The point we have repeatedly made to the ministers on
our courses has been: Why not face it that a different kind
of Church is appropriate for the 'urban priority area'? And
is that form of Church not an extra-parochial, non-denominational, post-denominational People's Church?

We have hardly ever got past the problem of agreeing
that to be the need. So we have hardly ever had to raise the
question of how it would get going – a quite separate
problem. But it is exactly what is needed.

Unfortunately, the People's Church is simply not in the
blood of the existing denominations. They have in fact all
but completely absorbed or extinguished the previous
elements of People's Christianity among the poor. The
denominations are funded by people in business and in the
suburbs, who put money into the denominations so that
they can set up missions, churches, or other work among
the poor. Native, indigenous, grassroots Christianity
among the poor has little hope of survival. The denominations now even have 'comity' agreements whereby one
denomination moves into one area and leaves another to
take a second area.

The Base Communities of Latin America[15] have advantages we lack. First, they have a lively sense of traditional, mainly Catholic, Christianity still present among the poor – and this is not the case with us. Second, there is a demand for Christian ministry among the poor that cannot be met by existing ministry or priests – which is not so in Britain. Third, unlike South America, for us the Church is neither the most likely nor the most obvious representative for the consciousness of the poor against their oppression – Britain has many other community and political organizations. Fourth, the pieces of denominational Christianity that we already have in poor areas are often outposts of an alien culture – again unlike South America.

Yet the People's Church is a vital part of the histories of some of our denominations. Guillermo Cook argues that the Base Church is very like Anabaptism, Congregationalism, Presbyterianism, and especially Methodism.[16] Cook also argues that Anglican and Roman Catholic churches do not belong to this tradition of people-led, primitive, Bible-centred, communistic and communitarian churches, which invariably begin in small groups of committed believers in a locality. Of course, the more recent adoption by the Free Churches in Britain of a basically Church of England style – which we observed at the outset – is part of their co-option into the straight society. But their theological, ideological and historical origins would draw them elsewhere, and the base ecclesial communities now remind them of their true origin and character.

More probably, the hope of a People's Church lies in a new inter-denominationalism or post-denominationalism. Perhaps we may see ecumenical task forces, orders of friars/sisters, people's preachers, or lay evangelists. Some at present in the British Base Communities might even be the means whereby such a new impetus in Christianity could take place. The two new-style Churches of the last two decades, the black Pentecostal churches and the house-church movement, might even show the way.

First, they are led by laypeople. Second, they are flexible in organization – the black Pentecostal churches in my area of Sheffield continue to rise and die and rise again under different names. Third, they begin in houses and only move into more public places when need arises and finance permits. Fourth, they are strongly materialistic and down-to-earth in their administrative style and decision-making processes – simply because the actual local participants and their available resources determine what is done, rather than some outside authority with outside funding.

Could there not be a People's Church that learned from this?

Certainly, twenty years in the inner city makes me long for a new movement in Christianity – of the people, for the people, led by the people. And confronting the existing Churches with another kind of Church – more nearly a Church of the poor, a Church of the Bible, a Church of Jesus.

NOTES

1 I summarize my *Radical Jesus*, esp. pp. 81–3. Basingstoke, Marshall Pickering, 1986.

2 J.J. Vincent, 'Mark's Gospel in the Inner City', in *The Bible and the Politics of Exegesis: Festschrift for Norman Gottwald*. New York, Pilgrim Press, 1991.

3 cf. J. Cassidy, *Jesus, Politics and Society*. Philadelphia, Fortress Press, 1982, and *Society and Politics in Acts*. Maryknoll, Orbis, 1985.

4 W.D. Morris, *The Christian Origins of Social Revolt*. London, Allen & Unwin, 1949.

5 C. Rowland, *Radical Christianity*. Cambridge, Polity Press, 1988.

6 cf. J.D. Davies and J.J. Vincent, *Mark at Work*. London, Bible Reading Fellowship, 1986. For example, pp. 21–34 on Mark 1 and 3.

7 L. Boff, *Ecclesiogenesis: The Base Communities re-invent the Church*. London, Collins; Maryknoll, Orbis, 1986; E. Schille-beeckx, *Church and Ministry*. London, Burns & Oates, 1988.

8 A study of these is lacking at present. But cf. a forthcoming work of John Munsey Turner.

9 J.J. Vincent, 'Basic Communities in Britain', in *Putting Theology to Work*, ed. D. Winter. London, Conference for World Mission, 1980, pp. 59–66.

10 J.P. Brown, *The Liberated Zone*. London, SCM, 1970.

11 J.J. Vincent, *Alternative Church*. Belfast, Christian Journals, 1976.

12 I. Fraser, *The Fire Runs*. London, SCM, 1975; M. and I. Fraser, *Wind and Fire*. Dunblane, Scottish Churches House, 1986; *Living a Countersign*. Glasgow, Wild Goose Publications, 1990. The Congress of Basic Christian Communities in Europe takes place every few years. The Congress of July 1991 in Paris 'is addressed to women and men having an experience with basis-groups or communities assembled to share their faith in basic Christian living for and with the marginalised of society'.

13 For the Ashram Community, see *What is the Ashram Community?* Sheffield, Ashram Community, 1985; for the Iona Community, see I. Fraser, *Living a Countersign*.

14 M. Walsh, *Here's Hoping. Heathtown, Wolverhampton and The Hope Community*. Sheffield, Urban Theology Unit, 1991.

15 The standard descriptive work is still *The Challenge of Basic Christian Communities*, ed. S. Torres and J. Eagleson. Maryknoll, Orbis, 1981.

16 G. Cook, *The Expectation of the Poor* (Maryknoll, Orbis, 1985), pp. 180–99, on 'Base Communities in the History of Protestantism'.

CHAPTER FIVE

Points of View

Transforming Inter-faith Relations

KIM KNOTT

In that wonderful children's book about nineteenth-century religion and timeless mystical experience, *The Stone Book*, we follow Mary as she pursues her father into the world of the stone mason.[1] Taking him his lunch one day, she climbs the tower and spire of Saint Philip's which her father has built, and there, from the weathercock at the very top, she looks out over North Cheshire to Wales and Manchester, 'and everywhere across the plain were churches. "Churches! I can see churches!" And all the weathercocks turned in the wind.' After that momentous experience, little knowing that something more extraordinary was yet to follow – and you must read the book to find out just what this was – she and her father climb Glaze Hill. 'When they reached the top the sun was ready for setting. The weathercock on Saint Philip's was losing light, and woods stretched out. "I can't see the churches", Mary said. "When we were up there this afternoon, I could." "That's because they are all of a height"', replied her father.

My interest here is the question of perspective. When you are of a height with the churches, you are aware of them, they are all around you, commanding your attention. When you look from above or below, they are lost in the surrounding landscape, their significance diminished. For Christians, the future of Christianity, whether in terms of its institutions or its gospel message, is central; for non-Christians, the view is different because the perspective, the point of view, is different.

There are, of course, many points of view, from the non-religious to the Muslim, the Buddhist to the Sikh, and so on. And within each of these categories, as within Christianity itself, there is a great diversity of opinion and experience. I am not able to speak *for* any of these. However, I can speak for the principle of many views, many voices, while knowing that my own cannot fail to come across.

This may seem hardly new in itself. However, I believe that despite the well-intentioned rhetoric of recent decades concerning religious and cultural pluralism that many white, middle-class people have used (myself included), it is the future that will bring a real opportunity to be challenged by diversity for reasons and in ways that are now beginning to emerge, the consequences of which might well be painful but the gains great. Currently, Britain and other Western countries are engaged in a lengthy phase of intellectual/ideological and spiritual re-evaluation.[2] This has been marked throughout by times not only of analysis and criticism, but of doubt and a shaking of self-confidence. For example, not infrequent is the disclaimer distancing contemporary white people from a part in slavery. But, of course, we are a part because we cannot choose as our heritage only that which we identify as good and wholesome. And this knowledge – of our part, our responsibility – and our desire to move towards a less guilty, more genuinely egalitarian future (begging the question of whether such a state of affairs is humanly possible), makes many of us fear our own assessments, our own point of view.[3] Personally, I see this as a good and necessary step, though it does not necessarily make for charismatic, powerful or rhetorical personalities or modes of expression. We may long for a messiah or leader, a rallying call, triumph, success, but can we trust ourselves with these any more? I am more inclined to expect the truth in pieces.

I want briefly to set before you some of the different points of view current now that might need to be heard as Britain hurtles towards 2020. They are not Christian points of view; they are the views of those of other religious perspectives resident in Britain today. There are many critical voices whose words are ignored at some peril, partly because those words represent other perspectives and also because they demand a response, a change. Some of those I have selected focus their attention on Christianity, others on different aspects of the dominant Western cultural and ideological system.

My own Jewish tradition becomes largely unintelligible when viewed in a liberal light. The first words of my Bible, 'In the beginning God created the heavens and the earth', are unproven and unprovable and so it can only be a private opinion, and an opinion that runs counter to the scientific principle that matter is self-creating, self-sufficient and eternal. A little later in the same chapter we read, 'And God saw that it was good'; the public realm of matter is neutral, without value, according to the canons of liberalism. And finally, at the end of the very first chapter of my Bible, it is stated that man is created in God's 'image and likeness', as opposed to the modern claim that man is an accidental product of evolution. It is not that liberalism presents my tradition with unanswerable challenges, but that it trivializes it and renders it unintelligible.[4]

Many committed Christian (and a few Jewish) writers assert, with a dramatic dogmatism as offensive as unfounded, that Muhammad selectively appropriated biblical ideas into the Koran and simultaneously enriched his version with a few curiously original incidents. . . . The Koran, it should be noted, explicitly claims to be the final and definitive edition of revealed scripture incorporating the truths of the Jewish and Christian dispensations, reopening the Ishmaelite lineage of sacred history, and in doing so, exploiting the prerogative of making appropriate addition and corrections. Muslims often need to shake Christian (and Judaic) complacency by explaining that Islam also possesses a scripture of integrity that embodies an autonomous expression of religiosity.[5]

So long as the blasphemy laws remain unrepealed they can be used; and so long as they can be used the Buddhist does not enjoy full freedom of expression. . . . There are sections of the Buddhist scriptures in which the notion of an omniscient Supreme Being is discussed by the Buddha and judged to be detrimental to the spiritual development of mankind. The terms used in this scripture may be deemed by some people to be 'indecent and offensive'. . . . Thus Buddhism itself may be deemed by some to be blasphemous and it would seem to be impossible to frame laws for the 'protection' of the theistic religions which do not by their very nature have this effect upon non-theistic religions.[6]

And, from 'an agnostic with a deep feel for the spiritual dimension of life':

. . . though all religions have talked about human brotherhood, they have defined and drawn the boundaries of brotherhood differently, and there is none that has admitted all men and women equally within its fold. For Christians Jesus is the way. For centuries they have argued that those who accept this tenet are privileged; those who accept Jesus as a way but not *the* way are at best step-brothers; those not accepting him even as a way are doomed if not damned. Islam too has its hierarchy of brotherhood and even a hit list. It privileges Judaism and Christianity, but has little mercy on the so-called idolaters, apostates and atheists.[7]

Finally, from an Indian woman speaking out against the dominant Western view of women in the subcontinent:

What,
white woman?
You say
I am
who?

Your
sister?
You have
a picture?
Me?
You have come to
help?
Why? When? How?
Here?

The picture,
white woman,
let me see it.
I remember no
picture
I gave you.
You have made a
picture of
me.
All by yourself.
Still,
let me see.

Indian woman.
Sati.
Child bride.
Dowry murder victim.
Traditional Hindu.
Untouchable.
Ostracized widow.
Traditional Muslim.
Wife No.1, No.2, No.3, No.4.
Raped.
Uneducated.
Illiterate.
Too many children.
Backward environment.
That's all?

Is that all,
white woman?
Is that me,
my sisters, my mothers? ...

Now
hear me speak
in my own voice,
GET OFF MY BACK.

GET OFF MY BACK,
for I am KALI
and will surely
destroy
all those who
trample on
Me.[8]

These all seem strikingly different: different themes, aims, objects of criticism. Each, however, concerns itself with voicing a minority perspective in relation to a more dominant religious or cultural system. In all there is a tone of injustice; in some, of fear, anger or insecurity. They show how hard it is to maintain one's faith location without indignation, accusation, with respect and integrity. These views are not intended to be typical. They are the voices of individuals, speaking out.

In recent years there has been an increase in the incidence of such voices; the *Satanic Verses* controversy encouraged many Muslims to speak out about the nature of their faith, their feelings of isolation, outrage, sorrow, etc. – for example, Rana Kabbani, Mashuq Ibn Ally, Zaki Badawi, and Shabbir Akhtar, from whose most recent book the passage on the Koran is taken. Muslims and Jews have defended their positions on ritual slaughter. Muslims have put the case for separate Muslim schools. Sikhs have spoken out for and against Khalistan, and Hindus and Muslims for and against the siting of the temple to Rama at

Ayoydha. These voices do not represent the whole faith community. All religious communities are made up of a range of opinions. In thirty years from now there are likely to be more such voices in evidence than now, not least of all because there is a growing recognition that there is a right and a need to speak, and a current intellectual unease with dominant voices, and the welcoming of previously unheard, minority perspectives.

The real question is: Do we as a society continue to hear these voices, often critical, in a spirit of toleration and sympathy but no more, or do we actually allow them to make a difference? If we want to do the latter, how do we honestly go about it?

One issue that needs considering before I come on to the major theme of my talk, the inter-faith process, is the inherent dynamism and independence of the various religious communities coexisting, but in a minority relationship, with Christianity. They will have their own ways of dealing with the future, probably a complex mixture of conservatism (necessarily inherent in all religions), and movements for change, adaptation and response to current circumstances both in British society and other relevant international locations. (Incidentally, this process is markedly different for those minority religious communities accustomed to experiencing racism or anti-Semitism.) Questions of leadership, sectarian development, the roles of women, the young and the old, relations with places of origin and their institutions, vernacular and sacred languages, educational and legal considerations, will all be important matters.[9] Currently, many groups are exploring issues related to future developments. Some examples of these are the session hosted last year by the Interfaith Network for the UK on young people in Britain's religions and the future, the development by Hindu sects of English language materials, by one Muslim sect of madrasah, by another of conferences and study sessions for the young, of Sikh youth camps. Slower in coming is the hard talk by those of different religions about what survival, growth and change actually mean in the context of Britain in the future (especially in a future inevitably also encompassing a certain amount of racism, anti-Semitism, Christian evangelism (a decade of it at least), and continued paternalism). What if it means sacrificing treasured verities or having them brought into question? What if it means losing valued languages, having young people question the role of rituals, having new styles of leadership? What if it means more doubt, more questioning, more compromise, more pain? There is a shortage of real discussion on these points (in Christianity too, of course). There are genuinely good reasons for this, particularly among those religions of postwar New Commonwealth settlers, because, as economic migrants, they focused on employment and community building rather than on theological reflection, religious self-examination and prophetic engagement. These later approaches are becoming more evident, however, particularly among younger members of the communities, or those who have had access to higher education.

Two commentators whose work, to my mind, is of greatest value in raising these issues are Shabbir Akhtar and Bhikhu Parekh. How much agreement there would be between them, I do not know. They certainly represent rather different religious positions (one a Muslim who might describe himself as a fundamentalist who is also a theological modernist, the other the 'agnostic with a deep feel for the spiritual dimension of life' cited above).[10] Their analyses, however, have some things in common, namely a call for more cultural autonomy, with responsibility, for different communities and a carefully constructed attack on many aspects of the ideological context of which we are all inheritors in Britain.

Shabbir Akhtar's new book, *A Faith for all Seasons: Islam and Western Modernity*, forcefully challenges the Muslim community or *umma*, particularly here, to face the task of opening up Islam to contemporary intellectual trends in the certainty that the outcome will be empowering. He presents himself as a scholar at the interface between his own religious community, to which he is deeply committed, and the dominant culture of modernity, and in doing this he reveals Islam and Christianity to one another, asking each to take the other seriously, but not with false tolerance or dishonest selectiveness. I will return to his critique of the current practice of dialogue a little later.

Bhikhu Parekh's contribution comes in the form of a number of refreshing and perceptive addresses on cultural and religious pluralism, inter-faith dialogue and the *Satanic Verses* controversy.[11] He has the advantage of being able to speak, as it were, from the outside on many issues – as an Asian agnostic – and he successfully mounts a critique of much liberal thinking and practice on issues related to community relations, multicultural activity and inter-faith work while suggesting new ways forward and novel goals. Of British identity, for example, he recommends a plural view, while not advocating, of necessity, shared values, a common view of history or the need to love Britain.

> Being British therefore means learning the grammar, vocabulary and syntax of the prevailing form of life and knowing how to participate in its ongoing dialogue intelligently and intelligibly.
>
> The cultural language is not static. It has undergone great changes in the past and is undergoing even greater changes today. ... Since the British way of life is conducted in a *common* language spoken in *different* accents, to be British is to be able to understand and handle the prevailing variety of accents. A white Briton who does not understand the cultural accents of his Muslim or Afro-Caribbean fellow-citizens is just as incompetently British as the Indian ignorant of the way his white fellow-citizens speak. In other words none of us is fully British. We are all constantly trying to become one. ... Only he *is* fully British who can honestly say that no British citizen, black or white, Christian or Hindu, is a cultural stranger to him.[12]

I bring these writers to your attention because, to my mind, their location outside white, Christian society (though they are both university educated, middle class and conversant through the former with Western liberal tradition) and their timely reflection on the way forward entitles them to be heard in a book committed to alternative points of view.[13] I cannot be where they are. None of us can do this in relation to another, though we can be empathetic to different perspectives.

Both these writers engage with the question of the interfaith process, and it is on this issue that I wish to focus the remainder of this discussion.

Two obvious ways of thinking about religions in Britain as they live alongside and relate to one another in the future are mission and dialogue. Both in terms of Scripture and history, the religions have formulated responses to one another, and in most, to a greater or lesser extent, theological evaluations have developed. There are just two points I wish to make about mission. First, that, though the Decade of Evangelism looks rather frightening from the perspective of other religions, such an event could conceivably provide a serious and challenging opportunity for religions to see one another honestly in their difference and 'strangeness', as the retiring Archbishop of Canterbury aptly put it in a recent talk.[14] Secondly, it is important to remember that other religions have their own concepts and practice of mission. Islam, Buddhism, the Baha'i faith and many other new religious movements are universal religions like Christianity with a mission to bring their message to others, though how they go about this differs according to religion, sectarian allegiance, geographical location and power relations. Bearing in mind the last of these, we can see that a Decade of Evangelism by Christians in a traditionally Christian country – albeit a much secularized one – is rather different to the missionary activities of a minority religion in such a context. Power and tradition do make a difference, both at the level of perception and in terms of persuasion.

Questions of power are of interest to me in relation to the second of the two modes of relationship, dialogue. It is this issue that I think we need to reflect on most in evolving successful strategies for the religiously plural future in Britain (indeed, in Europe as a whole, although there are many other social and political issues that need to be tackled responsibly alongside this – such as policies on immigration, asylum seeking, race relations, and suitable educational strategies). If we think of transactional analysis for a moment, we are reminded that, according to that account of relationships, we can behave to one another in a limited number of ways: child to child, parent to child and vice versa, adult to adult, etc.[15] To my mind, most of Christianity's dialogical relations with those of other religions have tended to be of the parent – I would go so far as to say 'father' – to child variety. Most parents, of course, are good and kind and loving, but they are also powerful. They think they know best. Children can withdraw their favours and be manipulative, but in most cases the rules and ultimate sanctions are in the hands of parents.

Let me not push this analogy too far, however. I mention it as a way in to talking particularly about the political and ideological location of inter-faith dialogue. (There are theological grounds to be considered as well, but space does not allow a discussion of these here.) Currently, we are just beginning to see the development of a critique of dialogue as it is currently understood and practised in line with similar recent critiques of orientalism, multiculturalism, the philosophy and theology of religious pluralism, and, to some extent, the disciplines of anthropology and religious studies.[16] There are issues specific to the critique of each, but, in addition, there is some common ground. All of these areas are rooted in Western traditions of colonialism and its aftermath, and liberalism. They were all well-intentioned pursuits and each was itself critical of ignorance, dogmatism, dominant monoculturalism and religious exclusivism, but none of these areas can escape, indeed all must come to terms with, their own histories and conditions if they are to continue to be useful and relevant.

I could not say when dialogue first began, though informally it has gone on for as long as there have been people able to articulate their faith. In India, for example, another country of religious plurality, it is known that there was much fertile discussion between ascetics of different persuasions at the time of the Buddha, that several centuries later the emperor Asoka, while spreading Buddhism far and wide in the subcontinent, exhibited a tolerant and engaging attitude towards other religions, and that the Mughal emperor Akbar, despite orthodox criticism, actively enjoyed meeting those of other faiths including Hindus, Buddhists, Zoroastrians and Christians. Moving on to the eighteenth and nineteenth centuries in India, we begin to see dialogue emerging as a component of British imperial relations with India. Looking back at that context, it is often hard to pick apart Christian mission and dialogue.

Why do I mention India? Because it is in that colonial context, I believe, that we can see the foundations of the contemporary dilemma concerning inter-religious and inter-cultural relations. Although some interest in encountering religions other than Christianity stems from the scholarly pursuit of an understanding of the exotic – and this would apply to William Jones and Max Müller in India and myself here and now – most interest is itself religiously motivated. Of this, some is part of a personal faith exploration, as in recent interest in Hindu new religious movements and Buddhism; the rest is part of a felt need by Christians to engage with faiths other than their own for mutual understanding, responsible outreach in a multi-faith society and for a deepening of their own faith. Incidentally, it is not my intention to suggest that these various interests do not overlap, or to claim for any of them superiority or freedom from a rootedness in colonialism.

Kenneth Surin says of religious pluralism, the philosophical and theological response to religious plurality, that it is the liberal corrective to orientalism.[17] Similarly, I would say that inter-faith dialogue is the liberal corrective to heavy-handed missionary activity and religious exclusivism on the part of Western, particularly British, Christians. I think there is probably something in this, as many former missionaries are now actively engaged in dialogue. In addition, the Christian organ for dialogue in Britain (the Committee for Relations with People of Other Faiths – soon to be replaced under the Council of Churches of Britain and Ireland) comes under the Conference for World Mission. They seem to be two sides of the same coin. What, if any, are the problems stemming from dialogue being such a liberal corrective? It is important to ask this now precisely because, for those involved in it, the value of inter-faith dialogue seems self-evident and this itself can lead to complacency and a failure to challenge current practices and assumptions for the future.

Anyone involved in dialogue will willingly concede that it is a minority interest that captures the hearts and minds of very few traditional, evangelical, mystically oriented or nominal members of different faith communities. In addition, not all, but many, are Christian, and it is almost always Christians who are responsible for founding groups and writing about the dialogical enterprise. Great efforts have been made to extend inter-faith activity into different religious communities, but these efforts have normally been made by Christians. I also believe that, as a result of the above, the agenda of dialogue is also Christian, though many issues discussed and activities performed may have increasing relevance to those of other faiths. I do not mean here just the content of dialogue, but also the need for dialogue. If dialogue is a corrective to old-style colonial missionary activity, it represents a felt need to do justice to those who were once fodder for conversion, a need perhaps to repent.

Do the other religions currently engaged in dialogue or being brought within the dialogical fold have the same need? Certainly not. I believe, in the British context, that one of the key needs for dialogue felt by those of other religions, minority religions, is the need for representation, an opportunity to speak and be heard, to obtain greater status and power, things that Christianity already has by virtue of its perceived size and position.[18] Building relationships can provide an opportunity to seek forgiveness; it can also provide an opportunity for getting on, gaining power. Currently, dialogue rarely confronts or meets these objectives and needs (although there are some exceptions, including the recently formed Interfaith Network which is trying to take some of these matters on board).

This failure to be clear about objectives and needs seems to be underlined by Shabbir Akhtar in his assessment of Christian–Muslim exchange:

> Muslims do sometimes suspect the motives of their Christian counterparts. And there may be grounds for suspicion. Why, after all, should Christians whose forefathers have opposed Islam root and branch, by means fair and foul, for well over a thousand years, suddenly wish to effect a peaceful reconciliation? This is an important worry. For the current liberal attitude towards Islam prevalent among some Christians is either the result of a betrayal of a principle held tenaciously for centuries or else it is a realisation of past errors. Neither of these possibilities is sinister: nations can sometimes owe allegiance to false ideals and do so for centuries; to realise one's errors or those of one's ancestors is an act of humility and, as such, worthy of respect. What is troubling, however, is the possibility that dialogue is merely part of a new strategy to deal with an old enemy. Could it be that some Christians are merely putting a different bait on the old hook? Could it be that dialogue is sometimes undertaken in deference to the maxim 'Know thine enemy'?[19]

If those involved in dialogue wish to take seriously the history and conditions that have brought it about, and do justice to the power relations that maintain it, greater

honesty and openness will be needed by all, and considerable humility and a release of the reins by Christian
participants. Questions about whether and in what way
dialogue serves the interests of those of other religions
(politically and theologically) need to be addressed. The
Zoroastrians, for example, resisted joining the Interfaith
Network because they felt it did not benefit them. No-one
can convert to Zoroastrianism, they said, so what was the
need of sharing information in dialogue? They would not
have wanted to lose members by the same token. Their
response indicates a most interesting perspective on the
relation of dialogue and mission.

The question of what dialogue might be like in thirty
years' time will depend to some extent on whether such
issues are taken seriously, on whether all the potential
participating voices are considered. Theological and moral
differences, even incompatibilities, will still provide enormous stumbling blocks and they will need to be tackled too,
but this is an older and more widely accepted criticism.
Considering all this, is dialogue worth the effort? What will
become of inter-faith relations if some of these points are
conceded and real changes made? What if some groups
freely decide it is not for them? Will other groups pick up
the reins if Christians withdraw to the sidelines? Will their
needs and interests in dialogue change if the power relations themselves begin to change?

No-one can be sure of the answers to these substantial
questions, but I believe that it is essential to take steps in
this direction for the sake of both political and social
justice, and the need to value genuine cultural and religious
differences. 'Letting go' is hard and responding to criticism
with change is a slow process, but I am hopeful, not least of
all because of movements on the intellectual front that are
bringing into question our ethnocentric orientation, Western imperialist leanings and failure to take seriously the
alternative voices.

There is a genuine fear among some about the logical
consequences of giving full rein to the interests of minority

religio-ethnic communities. Would a radical pluralism be the outcome in which different groups were permitted to pursue separately their own internal objectives, independently exercising customary practices (including laws), educating their children in separate schools, maintaining community languages to the exclusion of English, etc.? Is this the only way that contemporary concerns for racial, social and religious justice and equality can be met?

Personally, though I believe we must and will move further in this direction (this is already suggested by legal and educational trends), I do not see this scenario as problem-free.[20] One of my major fears would be the conditions of women in such a society. Equality of opportunity for women, theoretical freedom from harassment and prejudicial behaviour and the recognition of the distinct nature of women's voices – to some extent, these are gains obtained and given legal support in a liberal climate that will not necessarily be maintained in a radically plural society that raises the status of traditional religious or cultural communities (including Christian ones) at the expense of all centralized decision-making processes, common objectives and shared values.[21] (Liberalism has not, of course, been all sweetness and light for women. Androcentrism and paternalism have been inevitable features of its operation, and we saw its impact on non-Western women in the poem read earlier.) However, most of those who call for greater decentralization and the need for more recognition and independence for distinct groups accept the concomitant need for shared codes, representative bodies, protective legislation and the right for individuals to choose not to be judged part of a community that lays claim to them.[22]

Giving up on dialogue is not the answer for the future, though the process of the religiously committed from different communities meeting and talking should be seriously rethought. Perhaps Christians need to rethink their role in it altogether. This may be difficult while Christianity, especially the Church of England, is perceived by non-Christians to have political clout at all levels of society, but it is necessary. As John Vincent says in his chapter, the strong (middle class, educated, denominationally bound) cannot be successful mediums for the weak and poor. They cannot organize on their behalf either. Their message, their culture, becomes distorted. Similarly, Christians cannot successfully function in this way for those of other religions. Distortion again is the outcome. In fact, talking in Parekh's 'different accents' may well best be done in shops, clinics, playgrounds and on street corners, places incidentally frequented very often by women, women more practised than men in listening as well as speaking and perhaps more able to bridge cultural and religious chasms through their common experience of powerlessness. I would not like to see the inter-faith process left to the religious professionals, most of whom are men. I would like to see more 'doing' together as well as talking together – 'doing' in different accents because ends are more important than we sometimes give them credit for, and working together to make something practical is often a more realistic way forward than talking towards the more abstract end of mutual understanding. In addition, I would wish to see many more people – traditional, evangelical, mystical, nominal, liberal in all religions, and indeed the non-religious – in conversation with one another, even in disagreement and misunderstanding. This may be the first step away from silence, separation and a sense of isolation.

What is the likelihood of these developments coming to be thirty years hence? I do not know, though I think there is already an awareness concerning some of these issues that will stimulate change. I can only say that the process of thinking about the future, not least of all because the present is so bad, brings pain as well as hope, because it involves accepting the need to recognize and do something about issues of power from which so many of us continue to reap the benefits. Attempting to see the position and role of Christianity from other points of view and working to change the balance of power in the inter-faith process will be very hard, but, to my mind, it will be an honest step in the pursuit of truth, a truth necessarily in pieces.

NOTES

1 A. Garner, *The Stone Book*. London, Fontana Lions, 1979. In addition to those authors cited below, I am indebted to many of my colleagues and postgraduates for conversations on the subjects of religion and plurality, and dialogue.

2 See A. MacIntyre, *Whose Justice? Which Rationality?* London, Duckworth, 1988.

3 Debates in early 1991 on the Gulf crisis also reflected this questioning of dominant ideological positions.

4 P. Morris, 'Judaism and Pluralism: The Price of Religious Freedom', in *Religious Pluralism and Unbelief: Studies Critical and Comparative*, ed. I. Hamnett. London, Routledge, 1990, pp. 187–8.

5 S. Akhtar, *A Faith for All Seasons: Islam and Western Modernity*. London, Bellew, 1990, p. 183.

6 'Note on Blasphemy by the Office of the Western Buddhist Order', *Law, Blasphemy and the Multi-Faith Society: Report of a Seminar*. Discussion Paper 1, London, Commission for Racial Equality/The Interfaith Network for the United Kingdom, 1989, pp. 88–9.

7 B. Parekh, 'Who Are God's Children? Explorations in the Crisis of Religion and Modernity'. *World Faiths Insight*, New Series 25, June 1990, p. 14.

8 S. Thobani, 'Indian Woman'. *Bulletin of Concerned Asian Scholars*, 21:1, 1989.

9 See K. Knott, 'Bound to Change? The Religions of South Asians in Britain', in *Oxford University Papers on India, Volume II, Number 2: The Modern Western Diaspora*, ed. S. Vertovec. Delhi, Oxford University Press, in press.

10 S. Akhtar, 'Faith Should Be All or Nothing'. *The Observer*, 26 March 1989.

11 In addition to the articles cited elsewhere in these notes, see 'Between Sacred Text and Moral Void' (*New Statesman and Society*, 24 March 1989) and 'The Rushdie Affair and the British Press', in *The Salman Rushdie Controversy in Interreligious Perspective*, ed. D. Cohn-Sherbok. Lewiston/Queenston/Lampeter, The Edwin Mellen Press, 1990.

12 B. Parekh, 'Britain and the Social Logic of Pluralism' in *Britain: A Plural Society. Report of a Seminar*, Discussion Paper 3, London, Commission for Racial Equality/The Interfaith Network for the United Kingdom, 1989, p. 75.

13 This discussion of 'Christianity' treats that religion monolithically. I concede that, like all religions, it is comprised of many denominations, sects and styles and that I have not done justice to this diversity here. I feel it is particularly important to point out that I have failed to mention black-led churches. These bear a different relationship to the issues under discussion than do the mainstream denominations in Britain today.

14 R. Runcie, 'Archbishop's Address', Report of plenary meeting of the Interfaith Network held on 29 November 1990, London.

15 E. Berne, *Games People Play*. Harmondsworth, Penguin, 1970.

16 Examples would include the work of Edward Said and Rana Kabbani on orientalism, Edward Hulmes on multiculturalism, Kenneth Surin on religious pluralism, James Clifford on 'modernist' anthropology, and Shabbir Akhtar on the discipline of religious studies and on dialogue.

17 K. Surin, 'Towards a Materialist Critique of Religious Pluralism: An Examination of the Work of John Hick and Wilfred Cantwell Smith', in *Religious Pluralism and Unbelief*, p. 119.

18 Many Christians would deny that their religion has power and status in Britain today in view of the dominance of a secular culture and secular institutions. There is some truth in this, but, to non-Christians, Christianity is thought to have a powerful voice, particularly because of the traditional relationship between the Church of England and the state, but also because of its role in the voluntary-aided sector of education.

19 Akhtar, *A Faith for All Seasons*, p. 187.

20 For examples, see S. Poulter, 'Cultural Pluralism and its Limits: A Legal Perspective', in *Britain: A Plural Society. Report of a Seminar*; A. Allott, 'Religious Pluralism and the Law in England and Africa: A Case Study', in *Religious Pluralism and Unbelief*; E. Hulmes, *Education and Cultural Diversity*. London, Longman, 1989.

21 For a discussion of some of the issues, see N. Yuval-Davis and G. Sahgal, 'Refusing Holy Orders' (*Marxism Today*, March 1990) and C. Connolly, 'Washing Our Linen: One Year of

Women Against Fundamentalism' (*Feminist Review*, 37, Spring 1991).
22 For example, see Morris, 'Judaism and Pluralism', and Parekh, 'Britain and the Social Logic of Pluralism'.

CHAPTER SIX

A Humanist Perspective

Religion and the Politics of Morality

BERNARD CRICK

For a long time a debate has been waged between Christian and secular rulers on the question whether democracy is the product of the Christian faith or of a secular culture. The debate has been inconclusive because, as a matter of history, both Christian and secular forces were involved in establishing the political institutions of democracy; and the cultural resources of modern free societies are jointly furnished by both Christianity and modern secularism. Furthermore there are traditional non-democratic Christian cultures to the right of free societies which prove that Christian faith does not inevitably yield democratic historical fruits. And there are totalitarian regimes to the left of free societies which prove that secular doctrine can, under certain circumstances, furnish grist for the mills of modern tyrannies. The debate is, in short, inconclusive because the evidence for each position is mixed (R. Niebuhr, *Christian Realism and Political Problems*).

'The evidence for each position is mixed', indeed. Niebuhr famously wished to build bridges between the two positions. One bridge that he offered for 'a strong affinity ... between democracy and Christianity' was that 'the tole-ration which democracy requires is difficult to maintain without Christian humility'.[1] Perhaps that is one way of putting it; but in this context, 'scepticism' is often, if not an exact synonym for humility, at least an acceptable historical substitute. 'Modern morality', said the philosopher and social anthropologist Ernest Gellner, 'does in fact accord respect to honest doubt, rather than to ill-founded conviction.' But his remark also cuts in both directions, restraining Christian and humanist alike. Actually I'm not sure that modern morality does stop short of giving respect even to ill-founded convictions, so long as they are sincerely held (an exaggerated respect for sincerity and authenticity is what many have against modern morality). The breaking point between respect and rejection is not people holding ideas of any kind, but when they try to impose them on others.

I raise this theme of the ambiguity of tolerance by way of prelude; I will expand it later. But let me begin at the beginning, before Niebuhr's democracy and before the Christian revelation even, with the Greeks and the Romans. We need to consider the nature of politics itself, both philosophically and as something with a cultural history, therefore an origin; and an origin, both as speculation and as practice, no older than the Greek city states.

THE NATURE OF POLITICS

By politics, then, I mean exactly what Aristotle meant. It is an activity among free men living as citizens in a state or *polis*; how they govern themselves by public debate. Of course, even in Aristotle's great book (or rather lectures) *The Politics*, the word was used for any type of government as well as in this special sense. And the special sense to him was not necessarily, at any given time, democratic. A *polis* must have a democratic element in it, but he favoured mixed-government: the able rotating and governing with the consent of the majority (and even that excluded slaves, foreigners and women, of course). A pure democracy, he said, would embody the fallacy that because men are equal in some things, they are equal in all. However, the special sense of polis or civic state was to him a conditional teleological ideal: both a standard and a goal to which all states would naturally move if not impeded, as well they might be, by folly, unrestrained greed or power-hunger by leaders lacking civic sense, or by conquest – which finally settled the matter (as Machiavelli was to notice).

Aristotle brings out the intense specificity of the political relationship (and I will soon say its inherent secularity) when, in the second book of *The Politics*, he examines and criticizes schemes for ideal states. He says that his teacher Plato made the mistake in *The Republic* of trying to reduce everything in the *polis* to an ideal unity; rather, it is the case that

> there is a point at which a *polis*, by advancing in unity, will cease to be a *polis*: there is another point, short of that, at which it may still remain a *polis*, but will none the less come near to losing its essence, and will thus be a worse *polis*. It is as if you were to turn harmony into mere unison, or to reduce a theme to a single beat. The truth is that the *polis* is an aggregate of many members.

Politics arises then, according to Aristotle, in organized societies that recognize themselves to be an aggregate of many members, not a single tribe, religion, interest or even tradition. That is why in my *In Defence of Politics* I defined politics as the activity by which the differing interests and values that exist in any complex society are conciliated.[2]

Politics arises, then, from a perception of differences as natural. But this perception has both an empirical and an ethical component. The empirical component is a generalization that all advanced, complex or even (just say) large societies contain a diversity of interests – whether moral, social or economic; and in fact, usually blendings of each, hard to disentangle. The ethical component is that there are always limits beyond which a government should not go in attempting to enforce consensus or unity. Perhaps no limits can be demonstrated in general. They may all be specific to time and place. But the principle of *limitations* is general and the empirical distinction is usually clear, allowing for deceit, rhetoric and muddle, between regimes that strive to limit power and thus govern politically, and those regimes whose rulers strive after total or at least unchallengeable power. That my definition of politics, or rather Aristotle's, is not an empty truism can be seen at once if one sadly remarks that most regimes even in the modern world are not political: they hunt down politics, not encouraging it as a civic cult; they act politically only when faced with a superior, immovable or uncertain rival power.

Some call themselves 'realists' and say that politics is basically only and all about these differences of interest, a matter of 'conflict'. Hard-nosed political scientists might accept at least half of St Augustine's analysis: that any justice in the earthly city is simply self-interest. States hold together for the same reason that bands of robbers hold together: self-love and mutual interest. Others call themselves, or more often are called, 'idealists' and say that politics is basically about doing what is right: 'where there is no vision the people perish' or 'let justice be done though the heavens fall' (as is most surprisingly written over the main door of the Old Bailey). But beware of the fallacy of the excluded middle. It is possible to reject both: 'realism' for not allowing enough to at least occasional altruism and sociability; and 'idealism' for being prone to dangerous chimeras of human perfectibility. One does not have to be a Christian to hold a tender scepticism (or humility?) about human perfectibility. So a third school says that political morality is about reaching some consensus or agreement about civic procedures, about the institutional conditions of peace and justice, not about the nature of peace and justice themselves: political institutions should build a ring and hold it fairly in which all comers can debate and attempt to get their way (well, nearly all comers; not those who try to smash up the ring – as even John Stuart Mill agreed). As a *politique*, I am obviously of this third school.

You will notice that I have moved from talking of morality in politics to 'political morality'. I mean that it is the mark of politics that it often has to conciliate, in some manner that is both right and acceptable, rival codes of morality as well as material interests. This is close to what Kant meant by 'practical reason', or what Max Weber called an 'ethic of responsibility' rather than 'absolute ethics'. The first advocate of toleration as state policy, Jean Bodin, argued that it was not the business of the state to punish heretics, but only to keep the peace; but he also believed that God would damn them hereafter.

RELIGION AND POLITICS

If in considering the future in Britain, politics involves dilemmas for the religious, religions can also pose dilemmas for the political. A little later I must remind us that the whole concept of toleration (which is a curious concept anyway) arose no earlier than the seventeenth century in reaction to wars of religion. And it would be bad taste to dwell on the fact that these wars were not metaphorical and were among Christians. In the last twenty years I have attended numerous conciliation conferences or meetings, both open and clandestine, in or about Northern Ireland. In the fervour and fury of the new ecumenicity, a Catholic priest and a Presbyterian minister will commonly chant in unison, 'As we were the root and cause of this conflict, it is now for us to solve it together'. When I was bold enough to air an opinion, I would welcome the first part of the statement as historically more or less true and as removing some inhibitions in discussion, as well as for its possible therapeutic value to those who uttered it; but would then caution that the second proposition was at best a half-truth and, at worst, dangerous hubris. The gentler way of putting this is to say, as I know many Christians do, that one should do one's best, but not take on impossible burdens in society, in the *civitas terrena*. Many of you may feel that the *civitas dei* is entitled to a little spare energy and study.

The point I wish to make is that political activity, whatever its motivation, is a secular activity: the worse for that, said Augustine, only part of the fallen and transitory state of man carried away by the waters of Babylon; good enough, said Thomas Aquinas, part of natural law open to the reason of all mankind, Christian, Jew and infidel alike, even though, of course, it was incomplete without divine law and the bending of God in grace. Calvinists often said that the sphere of statecraft as such was something 'morally indifferent', although whether magistrates acted in a Christian manner was crucial. Christ's injunction was both broad and clear: 'Render unto Caesar that which is Caesar's and unto God that which is God's'. The principle is clear, even if the application makes it always what philosophers now call 'an essentially contestable concept'. None the less, it rules certain things out and thereby makes other things plain. Theocracy is ruled out, except as a heresy – however much images of the nature of God affect all our perceptions of the nature and purposes of political authority.[3] Christian theology, unlike some other world religions, is essentially dualistic: some things are one, some the other. They are not of equal value, but there is a division. Put in the simplest terms: Caesar must not dictate to God's servants and God's servants have no business dictating to Caesar on secular matters, at least not in God's name. As citizens they may do what they wish within the limits of Christian belief; but belief is neither a sufficient nor a sure guide in all political action. Unlike the authority of God, the authority of neither Church nor state are comprehensive, they are specific. And looked at from the point of view of individuals, the good life, the life of virtue, is no longer political or public life itself as in Greece and Republican Rome: it is a life of prayer, praise, striving for salvation and ministry, even though ministry also has duties towards works and the world stemming from the Beatitudes.

All I point out, from outside, and forgive me this banality, is that such good Christian injunctions as to help the poor, to love our neighbours and to honour the peacemakers, which would, indeed, have a totally transformative and revolutionary effect on political order if everyone acted according to them (which is unlikely both in common sense and by Christian views on human imperfection), these injunctions cannot be forced on people. They cannot be forced both in historical senses – we've never seen it work, only the bloodshed and the horror of forced conversions; and because in philosophical senses there is freedom of will, there is conscience and individuality. Minimally, if moral progress is to be made in removing or modifying legislation or behaviour unacceptable to Christians, this progress has to be through politics: convincing and compromising with unbelievers. Maximally, if any still wish to make progress towards a Christian commonwealth, the path must still be through persuasion; unless, as the more eschatological and less cautious of liberation theologians have sometimes suggested in South America and Southern Africa, there is sudden simultaneous mass conversion and changing of hearts. Well, perhaps. There is some ground for this in Christian tradition. But I don't think it reasonable or morally responsible to bank on it.[4]

Even in what seemed until very recently a quite desperate situation, South Africa, the preaching of mass transformation and revolution has now given way to political bargaining and the making of compromises. But, I must in all honesty say, many – perhaps most – of those involved are motivated by Christian principles (or painful rethinking in the Afrikaans seminaries). Yet it would be equally fair to say of apartheid – as Machiavelli said of Philip of Macedon, 'moving whole populations as if they were sheep and not men' – that 'one does not have to be a Christian to see that that was evil'.

It seems to me that it is very important for any group who wish to be taken seriously, be they a party or a church, an ideology or a sect, not to claim too much, always to shave close with great Occam's razor lest in claiming too much one imperils or renders incredible or ridiculous what is truly important. I am irritated, almost angered at times, by that shallow argument that without religion there can be no morality. The question arises, what religion? Or have a limited class of religions a common morality? Some may have some elements of a common theology, but that's a different question. And they all believe in salvation, more or less: views about the ontological status of non-believers do vary a bit. But (and I'll return to this point) it seems to me that if one gives to different religions, to different creeds of Christianity indeed, the respect deserved by the importance of their claims and the sincerity of their claimants, then one must see that different moral codes are involved. Think only of prescriptions on sex and the family – let alone punishment, property, inheritance, diet and drink.

It would be a long argument, but I am convinced that we all owe to each and every other person, simply in the capacity of their being human, a respect and recognition to another unique and equal individual. This is essentially H.L.A. Hart's view of what is involved in the idea of human rights – Hart a sceptic, differing greatly in grounding but not so much in conclusion from Immanuel Kant's categorical imperative; Kant a Christian, but by faith: morality he held must be a universal derivable from common reason.[5] The good metaphor that we are all brothers and sisters does not depend for its force on there being a father, or knowing who that father is or what his will. If you lost your faith in the Creator very suddenly, I would still feel safe in your company at dinner; and would not expect you to assume you'd be robbed by me because I am not a Christian. I am not a Christian. I lack faith. But intellectually I have always understood, as once I felt when younger, that Christianity is about matters even more important.

I do not hesitate to call things good or bad when moral choices or judgements are called for. Humanists often do themselves less than justice by trying to avoid what social scientists quaintly call 'value judgements'. I make them all the time; too easily sometimes. This drives some secularists either into a rigid utilitarianism, often trying to count up (or pretending to) unreflective public opinion on complex issues, or into a kind of pseudo-empirical rhetoric. This can come from both Left and Right. 'If something isn't done about unemployment, society will break down'; or if you take the *Daily Telegraph* rather than the *Guardian*, then substitute the word 'crime'. What they mean to say is that unemployment and crime are morally wrong; no way to treat people, no way for people to act. A few years ago even Lord Longford was arguing perfectly seriously that the spread of pornography would lead to the breakdown of British society. This was most unlikely. Even he got trapped in empiricist rhetoric. He surely meant that it was wrong, morally repugnant. On the whole, I thought so too. And I argued that if more secular liberals publicly said that porn was rubbish or sometimes intolerably offensive to – or actually threatening to – women, if there was more condemnation or mockery, there might have been less demand for legislation. Because something is morally wrong it does not follow that it should be banned.[6]

However, let me quickly say that a rational secular morality is either an affair of philosophers and intellectuals, demonstrating its possibility, or else of the kind of 'innate decency' (Orwell's words) that one still hopes to find in most ordinary working people. There is more sociability or mutual care among working-class neighbours than among the middle classes: capitalist society is like that. To judge by editorials even in the quality press, the old sense of a reasonably clear civic and secular morality is a declining faculty in the middle ground of the opinion makers or facilitators. It lacks institutions and organizations. There was once a feeling that the Labour Party embodied the old non-conformist conscience (which Max Beerbohm said 'makes cowards of us all'). But that is an even longer generation ago than when the Conservative Party was openly and unashamedly paternalistic. Both the parties now seem scared of speaking with any other language but that of economic self-interest. And material interests are, remember, indeed half of the political equation but only half: values *and* interests, interests *and* values. So it seems to me that the Churches, for reasons quite unconnected with theology, probably far less connected with personalities than is thought, and hardly deliberately, got drawn into what I hope (I nearly said pray) is this temporary vacuum.

The report *Faith in the City* has to be seen in this light. It would never have had much notice or caused such a storm in press and Parliament if the Labour Party had not seemingly abandoned its good old moral rhetoric (out of fear that every time it said anything moral people would feel the taxman's hand in their pocket). They yielded the moral high ground and descended to the battlefield offered by their opponents: that of who will give or take more from whom. In such a decline of genuine political thinking, almost by default the Churches began to sound like an effective political opposition. It was churchmen who stated the obvious moral case for the social justice of retaining a steeply graduated income tax – though that is a matter of common morality, not specifically Christian. Hence the counter-attack from newly theologized noisy MPs, and the equal danger to the true role of the Church of, on the one hand, John Selwyn Gummer's and Enoch Powell's obsessive 'Keep Out: no works, only faith' or, on the other hand, of Frank Field's conviction that the Labour Party still marches in a mysterious way towards the New Jerusalem and the Kingdom.

TOLERATION AND PLURALISM

I was taught at the London School of Economics by Harold Laski, an agnostic Jew who preached a socialist version of philosophical pluralism explicitly based on the Anglican divine J.N. Figgis's *Churches in the Modern State*. For churches, we knew that Laski was substituting trade unions when he intoned, 'a free church in a free state'.[7]

But that analogy in political terms, and this must include the churches when they are involved in political issues, is not a bad one. And now not just a plurality of Christian churches in Britain, but of religions: now Hinduism and Islam as well as Judaism. The internal tensions created by the terrible war in Iraq and the Rushdie affair are still in all our minds. And religion and ethnicity unhappily but quite obviously, if contingently, go together. And if you who are living in England now have to start thinking of Britain as a pluralistic society, religiously, non-religiously and ethnically, you had better also start remembering the Scots, before by insult or neglect they begin acting somewhat like the Northern Irish, whom we would willingly forget if we could. The Welsh are another question again, having an intense sense of common identity, but either two identities overlapping or one with a formidable linguistic division. Now in a sense this was always so, for three centuries at least. The real question is why the English did not recognize it and, at least in popular consciousness, celebrate the pleasures of variety in a state composed of four nations, not one. Life might have been easier for the new immigrants if their cultural diversity could have been seen as not raising in principle any essentially new problems of administration and popular tolerance, but ones analogous to those of the four nations and the once open hostilities between Christian Churches. Why should the immigrants be asked to be English? They may reasonably be required to be British. The one is a cultural identity, the other is a political and legal set of allegiances. The Scots are Scottish and British, not Scottish and English. But until the English have sorted out this distinction (in which the Anglican community should have a lot of experience to offer), the immigrants are in confusion.[8]

Reacting against the religious disputes of the seventeenth century, toleration both as a state policy and an educated attitude began to spread in Britain in the eighteenth century. But let us remember one essential thing about tolerance. It arises because people do differ on fundamental and important things, but wish to limit the practical effect of their differences. Tolerance is not complete acceptance, still less permissiveness; it is modified disapproval.

If you will forgive a humanist for saying so, I think ecumenicity can be taken too far. I was once privileged to hear the late General Eisenhower invoking 'our common Graeco-Romano, Christian-Jewish tradition': and nowadays his speech-writers might think to mention Black Muslims if not all of Islam. That is just what 'The Trimmer' John Savile, Lord Halifax, called – thinking of a pulpit of his day – 'good stout resolute nonsense'. Theologians today can do better. I wonder? Or are they just better behaved towards each other, which God knows is something. If I understand anything of the meaning of many doctrines of the Catholic Church and the somewhat less precise, which is also to say less dogmatic and inflexible, beliefs of the Anglican Communion, it seems to me beyond reason for theologians to hope to resolve or compromise such differences in committee – except either by negotiated surrender or by the somewhat unpredictable course of what I gather some call progressive revelation. And why should they? Surely what is much more important and plausible (both morally and politically) than seeking to synthesize dogmas is to gain greater understanding and respect by ordinary church members, not least in Ulster, of each other's *differing* beliefs. At least myth and fantasy might be dispelled. Toleration does need at least some cognitive element. I mean that if one doesn't know what offends others, much accidental offence can result when strongly held creeds coexist in close geographical proximity. Oiling the muskets with pig grease (if that did have anything to do with the Indian Mutiny – a lot of the facts we were taught were wrong facts) shows symbolically at least how specific and unexpected things can get. Try offering a meal to an orthodox Jew. Try reasoning with him about the dietary laws of Leviticus. Why bother? Learn and respect his odd different ways so as to plan intelligently how to deal with meetings. Of course, some reciprocity and mutual empathy helps. This is not always forthcoming from fundamentalists (the word 'fanatic' seems out of favour). And there are perhaps some limits to how long it is wise to go on turning the other cheek.

Toleration does not mean that we should search for the highest common factor or the least common multiple of all respectable beliefs, and end up with a kind of entromorphic ecumenical Muslim–Christian–Hindu–Buddhist–Holistic unitarianism. We should argue for our rival views of truth and morality vigorously but, yes, tolerantly. And always remember that it is sceptics and opponents we need to convince; preaching to the already saved is a largely useless pleasure. Britain has to become a more and more pluralistic society in every way. This does not mean watering down. It means a greater appreciation of differences and variety. Naturally in any society there are limits to toleration. Not all religious practices are acceptable to other groups, still less to majority opinion. But these limits have to be discussed politically: the will and the example must be there to reach creative compromises about behaviour, of course, but never about belief.

INCONCLUSIONS

It seems to me pointless and needless for my fellow British humanists to rail against the truth of religious beliefs, only against the abuse of authority (although I admit that the questions of religious broadcasting and of disestablishment do not 'warm my blood like wine', as the Greek anthologist put it, nor seem to me of the highest priority; though in another place I would vote on these issues in the way they have a right to expect of an honorary associate). It seems to me more important in these needlessly cruel and growingly materialistic times to assert the virtues of an active and participant common citizenship and civic morality, the modern form of the Aristotelian politics of creative compromise, and to cultivate a politics of moral judgements as well as of material interests working with any who think similarly. And we do this not as an ultimate end in itself, but as a necessary condition in which free lives and good lives can be cultivated.

Orwell, an agnostic, once said that socialists should not claim to be perfectionist, 'perhaps not even hedonistic':

> Socialists don't claim to be able to make the world perfect: they claim to be able to make it better. Any thinking Socialist will concede to the Catholic that when economic injustice has been righted, the fundamental problem of man's place in the universe will still remain. But what the socialist does claim is that the problem cannot be dealt with while the average human being's problems are necessarily economic.[9]

From what I have seen of conciliation groups in Northern Ireland, of university settlements, of members of charities and voluntary bodies working in inner cities among the poor, the destitute, the mentally handicapped decanted to 'the community', drug addicts or sufferers from AIDS, Christians are much more in evidence than my version of the silent majority: Orwell's ordinary people who have no faith but have a sense of common decency, fraternity, sociability, fellow-feeling, call it what you will. This, of course, is only an impression; there certainly are old-fashioned public-spirited humanists in this work, still vigorously counteracting the residual tendency of the Salvation Army to trade soup for souls. And there is the new breed of young professionals with Social Administration diplomas, often a puzzling mix of positive altruistic motivation and negative determination against jobs in business. I don't know whether Christians are more evident in the hard-edge of voluntary work because they are Christians, or simply because they are better organized. To me it doesn't matter. They don't question that one is just working for one's fellow men. I don't question in practice, only intellectually, what the priorities of churchmen should be.

None of these questions is easy. Niebuhr asked, in the extract at the beginning of this chapter, whether democracy owed more to Christianity or to secularism. He answered his own question inadequately when he said that mixed evidence produces an inconclusive debate. We are not dealing here with a debate that could or should lead us to choose between Christianity and secularism as the source of democracy. Both are necessarily and plainly present in democracy, which arises from their interaction. The dualism of Christianity allowed the fame and memory of the citizen tradition of the Greek *polis* and the Roman republic to survive. Civic republicanism was not always particularly honoured by Christians until long after the Reformation, but it was not always suppressed. It was the ideal definition of a secularity, the realm of Caesar, that did not challenge (or need not) the realm of Christ. The coincidence of the Renaissance and the Reformation gave these ideas of the scholars and humanists a wider circulation and an unexpected relevance. They were not, of course, democratic. Niebuhr forgot that. Aristotle thought that inherently only some *men* were fit to be citizens, and even the seventeenth-century republicans, while they saw no necessary limitation, advocated or assumed formidable barriers of education – which involved leisure and therefore the possession of property and income. It was when republicanism and Protestantism became involved with each other that the Christian belief in the spiritual equality of man (not equality in much else at that time, heaven knows) took on a political dimension. The first person actually to argue that every human being has a right to be a citizen simply by virtue of being human, not even educated – indeed, better to be simple, uneducated and natural – was Jean Jacques Rousseau, hating and hated by the Catholic Church but deeply influenced by Protestantism, a kind of crypto-proto unitarian.

A friend of mine who is, I must admit, an Anglican priest, seems to have got the balance and the tension about right. This is a long passage, but it has an interesting twist:

> The church [of England] does not have answers to all the problems the world sets itself. Its proper role is not to

aim at being relevant ... nor to conciliate on all occa-
sions, nor to 'influence society'. Its role is to proclaim the
judgment, the justice, the love of God, and to co-operate
with Him in the transformation of this world. In this
respect the concerns of the church are otherworldly. The
church should not reflect current values and trends, but
exists to question and challenge them. Rather than
attempting to answer current political questions, Christians might profitably contest the assumptions made by
the questioner and examine the terms in which the
question is posed ...

Church leaders do not have some privileged access to
political and social realities. ... Church leaders and
synods should not feel obliged to make a statement on
every issue of public concern. The misguided notion that
they are so obliged leads to the half-baked, mealy
mouthed and ambivalent character of many ecclesiastical
pronouncements. It is tempting to say therefore that
church leaders should speak only of general principles
and basic values, eschewing at all costs the particular.
For two reasons this position is unsatisfactory. First,
Christian moral judgment is made initially in the con-
crete case. The adequacy of a principle is assessed on the
basis of the particular actions it entails. Secondly, bishops can talk till they are blue in the face about general
principles, but with no discernible effect. It is when they
speak of particulars – the miners' strike, economic sanctions for South Africa, the forcible repatriation of the
boat-people – that people sit up and listen.[10]

Dr David Nicholls starts with a theological point, the
priority of witness; then points out that bishops have no
special authority in politics, but ends, startlingly to some,
by advocating highly specific interventions. Yes, politics is
like that: principles have to be applied to be meaningful.
And the church is not a trade union, but it is as much part
of the world as, indeed, a trade union. That is not, I
recognize, its primary role. But the interventions of the

churches are unavoidable, and often have some special merit; yet political acts even of churches are to be judged by political and secular standards. Politics cannot be divorced from morality; but it is the very *existence* (not the truth) of different moralities that is part of the origin of politics and part of its continual mediating process. If I read Niebuhr's version of Augustine right, there are two worlds to be judged by different standards; but the Church is in each of them. It is part of modern society and nobody should pretend otherwise, whether canons of Christ Church, former Prime Ministers or my fellow humanists. Recently, the churches have been drawn more into politics than they might intend by the politicians forsaking moral discourse entirely for a discourse of interest, and then savaging all those who seek even to restore a traditional balance. But I believe that for limited but important purposes there is much common ground to work upon between Christians and humanists if the future of British society is not to become as bad as one might rationally fear.

NOTES

1 R. Niebuhr, *Christian Realism and Political Problems*. London, Faber, 1954, pp.94 and 101.

2 B.R. Crick, *In Defence of Politics*, 2nd edn. Harmondsworth, Penguin, 1982.

3 D. Nicholls, *Deity and Domination: Images of God and the State*. London, Routledge, 1989.

4 J.J. Degenaar, 'Philosophical Roots of Nationalism' in T. Sundermeier, ed., *Church and Nationalism in South Africa*. Johannesburg, Raven Press, 1975.

5 H.L.A. Hart, *The Concept of Law*. Oxford, Clarendon Press, 1961.

6 B.R. Crick, *Crime, Rape and Gin: Reflections on Contemporary Attitudes to Violence, Pornography and Addiction*. London, Pemberton, 1974.

7 H.J. Laski, *Studies in the Problem of Sovereignty*. London, Oxford University Press, 1917.

8 B. Parekh, 'Britain and the Social Logic of Pluralism', in *Britain: A Plural Society*. London, Commission for Racial

Equality, 1990; and B.R. Crick, 'Englishness and British-
ness', in B.R. Crick, ed., *National Identities and the Constitution*. Oxford, Basil Blackwell and the *Political Quarterly*,
1991.
9 G. Orwell, in a *Tribune* 'As I Please' column, reprinted in *The
Collected Essays, Journalism and Letters of George Orwell*, vol.
3. London, Secker & Warburg, 1968, p. 64.
10 D. Nicholls, 'Politics and the Church of England'. *Political
Quarterly*, April–June 1990, pp. 141–2. This is a special
number on 'The Political Revival of Religion: Fundamentalists and Others'.

CHAPTER SEVEN

Trying to Get Well

*Trusting the God who Breaks in from
the Future*

MONICA FURLONG

When I suggested the title of 'Trying to Get Well' for this
chapter, I had, of course, no idea that within just a few
months the human sickness would have passed into such an
acute and frightening stage – the outbreak of the Gulf War
– and that the havoc wreaked by the passions of anger and
misunderstanding and greed, and the havoc that war
spreads around it in terms of physical injury and psychological agony, together with the gross injury to and agony of
the environment, would have become so terrifyingly plain.

I don't want to write directly about war here – partly
because it is such a vast and overwritten subject, such a
huge and disheartening projection of all our failures, that I
only feel able to approach it obliquely, trying, in minute
particulars, to catch the onset of tragedy in a less terminal
phase. As a Jewish teacher said long ago – when we strike
our brother or our sister it is as if we should use our own
hand to strike ourselves – a fairly futile endeavour. Yet the
illusion of separateness that brings about violence and war
is one to which all of us subscribe; alienation *is* the human
disease.

I am also conscious that I am writing at the beginning of
the Decade of Evangelism. Obviously, the Decade is the
churches' attempt to achieve the act of health and healing
that I have referred to in my title, but, as I hope I will
suggest in the course of this essay, I feel that the Decade
sets about it in far too shallow and prescriptive a way. The

real operation of healing, if healing is possible, seems to operate much more deeply and mysteriously. I would like to see us pointing people to the heart of the unknown mystery rather than, as I believe the Decade is in danger of doing, pointing them to a simplicity and safety and certainty that do not begin to meet the complexity of general bewilderment, and our own bewilderment as Christians.

So I would like to make it clear at the outset that I do not write with any sort of certainty, but only as a person who is groping for a few hesitant clues about where she feels food and comfort, energy and insight are to be found.

I feel that the human condition is rather like being a fly crawling slowly over a huge and complicated pattern on the wallpaper and trying, from this point of disadvantage, yet also of immediate experience, to calculate the appearance of the whole. Because I am relatively intelligent, the one thing I am quite sure of as I crawl is that I do not perceive the overall pattern accurately, though some bits of it I know with extraordinary intimacy. However, since this is the only first-hand evidence I have on which to base my suppositions about life, theology, my fellow-beings, the Church, God, it is no good being too tentative, though it is inevitable that I shall get a lot of things wrong.

Anyway, let me tell you some of the things I observe as I crawl; if others supply their observations perhaps we can arrive at a more cogent view. Although I am confining myself to my observations about Christianity, and in particular to its potential as a healing agent for the sicknesses of the human soul, it is the whole human condition that interests me. For when human societies and religion interact successfully, that is to say without bigotry or persecution or excessive moral rigidity, but rather imaginatively and creatively, then we have something like the condition for health.

Perhaps before I go any further, I should attempt some definition of health. I suggest a sense of joy, of well-being, of spontaneity, of relative security, of free-flowing energy, of zest for life, of an appetite for all the good things of life that operates without greed and without guilt. Along with an extraordinary capacity for curiosity, and pleasure and enjoyment, I would suggest an ability to develop insight, perception and intimacy – with fellow human beings of both sexes – and with the creatures, animal, vegetable and mineral, that form our world. Also, an ability to work creatively with the contradictoriness of life, to weave our experience of loss, of suffering, of pain, and ultimately of dying, into the joy and the appetite, the curiosity and the wonder of things.

Now I don't know about you, but that is scarcely a description of the person I have turned out to be, shot through with all sorts of stresses and fears, capable of waking at 3 a.m. and wondering how I am going to placate my bank manager, or of going back over disappointments that happened forty years ago and dramatizing myself as a quintessential victim.

Yet what we are talking about here is not so much our private inadequacies, but rather what I suggest Christians are talking of every time they celebrate Holy Communion – that is, the tracing of the pattern of things, the pattern of how things are that we keep losing and forgetting, and yet which, when we recover it, lends us some vision, some recollection of who we are and where we come from. The fly crawling up the wallpaper has the mystical experience of knowing something that she did not know she knew. There is a Hasidic story of a child who was taught a special tune in his native village. When he grew up and went out into the world, the rabbi said to him 'Don't forget the tune. But if you do forget it, then come right back home and learn it all over again.'

What is the pattern or the tune that we have lost – that sure sense of identity and discovery that has marked the best of Christian living? One of the recurring features of the pattern is a sense of all the apparent multiplicity of life being joined together somewhere, somehow, into one whole. A few weeks ago, at the British Museum, I was allowed to handle something called a churinga that had belonged to an Australian Aboriginal tribesman some ninety years ago. Australian Aboriginal peoples, so far as we can judge, have led a life with a rich sense of connectedness. They feel connected not just to each other, but also to the earth whose property they believe they are (unlike our Western idea that the earth is owned by us). They are connected too to all the animals and birds and plants around them, with many of which they share a sense of empathy, a spiritual bond that is supported sometimes by the eating of these sacred creatures. The land itself is supported by its human subjects by being repeatedly 'sung' into existence. Individuals carve for themselves a very holy object called a churinga, upon which they engrave the most relevant religious symbols – that is to say, symbols that for them spell life, meaning and health. The churinga I examined most closely was carved out of soft red wood on both sides and depicted innumerable concentric circles, all of them joined to other sets of concentric circles, so that the whole was a vast pattern of interconnectedness. Looking at this precious object with my blunted Western eyes and sensibilities, I could yet see one thing – that the person who carved it did not feel isolated, but part of some rich pattern of belonging: to his family, his tribe, to the world that began under his feet and stretched away in front of him. It caused me to ask what I would carve if I was asked to express my spiritual essence on a piece of wood.

The churinga brought home to me rather vividly the poverty of the civilization of which I am an heir. It has great wonders and riches of its own, but few of its children have such an overpowering sense of themselves as members of a whole; indeed, many are overwhelmed with the sense of loneliness and loss, of forms of alienation that drive them into illness and breakdown, into addiction and suicide.

I do not myself think it sufficient in the face of the psychological suffering so evident in our society to preach a return to family values, or a turning to the Lord Jesus as a quickfix solution to human agony. Our family life or our fantasies about the Lord Jesus are themselves limited and contaminated by our failure and sickness, so that we may find ourselves recommending a cure – a practice not uncommon in orthodox medicine – whose side effects are as grave as, if not worse than, the original sickness.

There is a need to go beneath and behind and around our glib solutions to our terrible problems and perhaps select a much simpler and more primitive strand from the human heritage – the strand of wonder is the one that I suggest. Something that we observe in young children, and some of us remember from our own early childhood, is a capacity to find the world wonderful, to be reduced to breathless astonishment and joy by a flower or a tree or a stone, by something that shines or that emits a noise, by a vision of running water, or snow, or cloud or sun, by the movement of an animal or the flight of a bird, by the ringing of a bell or by the thump of a drum. Hidden in this experience, I suggest, is something even more wonderful than wonder, which is a capacity to find the world and the people in it sometimes numinous – to the baby at the breast the mother is numinous, to a child caught up in seeing its first Christmas tree the smell and the fragments of light and the brilliant colours are numinous, to a slightly older child a fairy at the pantomime may be numinous, to an adolescent or adult the person they are in love with may be numinous; it is only among those who have become dried and disappointed in life that numinosity is to be sought only in a direct experience of God. Our whole world shines with sacredness and we have forgotten how to see it; we have to learn from children, artists and primitive peoples for whom it has not yet become necessary to put God into a sort of isolation hospital.

If we find the world wonderful we shall become reluctant to destroy it – we shall feel with the Red Indian that we would as soon rape our mothers as desecrate the earth itself who is also our mother.

So how do we, so cold, so rational, so sensible, so alienated, so greedy, rediscover a lost wonder in our beautiful world, the absence of which is rapidly turning our planet (which physicists say is made out of stardust – a magical substance if ever there was one) into a lifeless desert? The way to wonder is by cherishing, by nurturing, by enjoying, by taking time, by taking care, by contemplating, by fingering lovingly, by embracing, by observing gratefully, by copying, by imitating, by making jokes about, by sharing, by sacrificing ourselves joyfully, by singing to, by telling stories to and about. In just such a way, and with just such attention, have women cared for babies, have helped the process of life to continue upon earth in the face of every sort of hardship, difficulty and suffering, because life itself is the fundamental root of numinous awe reaching down into whatever it is that we call God – and blowing our minds at what God must be like if God is the womb out of which life emerges.

If we are to find our way, as I think we must if we are to survive, towards wonder, towards a sense of the world as numinous and sacramental and awesomely beautiful, towards a passionate cherishing, then we are talking supremely about feeling, and about learning to trust feeling. Our tendency has been to suspect feeling as leading into chaos, and to trust reason as leading to control, to choose the Apollonian rather than the Dionysian path. Yet by the bizarre contradictoriness of things, it is perhaps our rigid faithfulness to the Apollonian path that has brought us near to destruction – by technology, by abstract thinking, by common sense so rational that it becomes unexpectedly demonic, by laboratory formulae – and it is our neglect of Dionysus that has robbed us of joy and connectedness.

Feeling is about the here and now – it is about this moment when I feel the wind blowing, the rain on my face, the kiss on my lips, the sense of hunger, and of hunger satisfied, this sudden pain, that moment of drowsiness, this smell, that flash of sunlight, that feeling of cold, that touch of hardness, this stroke, that blow.

125

Feeling is about supreme moments of joy and it is also about devastating suffering. One reason that many, perhaps all of us, learn early in life to block out feeling is in a vain attempt to save ourselves from unbearable suffering. But if we block out suffering, we also block out connectedness. A religion that is to help us realize our full human potential has to realize both the value of chaos, of ecstasy, of the extraordinary sense of the oneness of the world that can come to us in this way, and also to have special insights about suffering so that we can work creatively with our loss, disappointment, bereavement, sickness and old age.

Our denial of feeling is often connected with the sense that anger is wicked, and since we all feel a lot of anger we are tempted to do a sort of Procrustes' mutilation to large parts of our personalities. The American feminist writer Beverly Harrison says this of anger:

> We Christians have come very close to killing love precisely because we have understood anger to be a deadly sin. Anger is not the opposite of love. It is better understood as a feeling-signal that all is not well in our relation to other persons or groups or to the world around us. Anger is a mode of connectedness to others and it is always a vivid form of caring. . . . Extreme and intense anger signals a deep reaction to the action upon us. . . . To grasp this point – that anger signals something amiss in relationship – is a critical first step in understanding the power of anger in the work of love. Where anger rises, there the energy to act is present. . . . Anger – no more than any other set of feelings – does not lead automatically to wise or humane action . . . but it is a signal that action is called for, that transformation in relation is required.

Can anyone doubt that the avoidance of anger in popular Christian piety, reinforced by a long tradition of fear of deep feeling in our body-denying Christian tradition, is a chief reason why the Church is such a conservative, stodgy institution? I suggest, however, that while many of us actually hold out little hope for the moral renewal of the Christian Church in our time, we are reluctant to face the cause of moral escapism in the Church – namely, the fear of feeling, and, more specifically, fear of the power of anger. We need to recognise that where the evasion of feeling is widespread, anger does not go away or disappear. Rather, in interpersonal life it masks itself as boredom, ennui, low energy, or it expresses itself in passive-aggressive activity or in moralistic self-righteousness and blaming. Anger denied subverts community. Anger expressed directly is a mode of taking the other seriously, of caring. The important point is that where feeling is evaded, where anger is hidden or goes unattended, masking itself, there the power of love, the power to act, to deepen relation, atrophies and dies.

Martin Buber is right that direct hatred (and hatred is anger turned rigid, fixated, deadened) is closer to love than to the absence of feeling. The group or person who confronts us in anger is demanding acknowledgment from us, asking for the recognition of their presence, their value. We have two basic options in such a situation. We can ignore, avoid, condemn, or blame. Or we can act to alter relationship toward reciprocity, beginning a real process of hearing and speaking to each other.[1]

It is not very surprising that this insight about anger and feeling comes from a feminist source, because for a good many years now Christian feminists have tried to use their anger creatively within the Church structures, and have discovered just what it means to be ignored, avoided, condemned and blamed, as well as being ridiculed, described as strident, aggressive and unfeminine. Recently a Fr Broadhurst proposed a motion in the General Synod of the Church of England saying that feminism is incompatible with the name and nature of God as revealed in the

Scriptures, and set out in the formularies and creeds and traditions of the Church of England.

It is not, of course, only the feminists who are angry. There has been every sign of suppressed and denied anger among the opponents of feminism, and a refusal to use this special opportunity to examine the issues that lie beneath the many forms Christian rejection of woman has taken: the fear of the body and its feelings; the fear of relationship; the temptation to use spirituality as an escape from bodiliness and the proper claims of sexuality; the need to dominate – women, children, the natural world, other nations.

How tragic that the Churches, and this applies almost as much to the Churches that ordain women ministers as to those who refuse, will not take this on as a part of the salvation of us all, to work towards reciprocity and mutuality with women rather than authoritarian bullying.

Those of us who have struggled hardest with this issue find it difficult to listen to the Pope, Dr Runcie, and other church officials who have prescribed listening and generosity as the way through the chaotic anger of the Middle East when, in the easier and less tortured climate of our own backyards, a different and far less incandescent anger is systematically ignored or blamed.

The issue of feminism has driven many women and some men to the fringes of the institutional Church. I have spent a good deal of time with these new groups and the most obvious thing about all of them is the emphasis on participation. They are places not unlike the house churches of which John Bunyan was a member – where everyone may speak, where everyone does speak, where the Bible is read and talked about, where new ventures in language and liturgy are normal as new experience tries to break through into speech, where many subjects you don't often hear discussed in church – violence against women, work problems, child problems, housework, money, vegetarianism, structures, authority – are aired, as well as others that are more usual like pacifism, homosexuality and divorce. In some there is a separatist tendency, as women seek a safe space in which to be themselves, in which in a real sense to discover themselves, since they have so often been told who they should be that it is difficult to know who they really are. In others there is a real effort to articulate some of the ways in which men and women fail to appreciate and understand one another. In all there is a recognition of a devastating background of violence, and a limiting of women's intellectual, economic, emotional and human potential, of the centuries in which they have been deprived of education and personal freedom, of the connivance of Christianity in this, condemning them to be silent for nearly 2,000 years. There is so much more life in these young groups than in the institutional Churches, that it is difficult not to see the churches, with their costly plant, their bankrupt cathedrals, their dead weight of palaces, and historic houses, and medieval buildings, their dubious political affiliations, as a hopelessly arthritic dinosaur that sooner or later is doomed. Meanwhile, the little animals, so quick on their feet, so alert to ideas, so acrobatic, and sometimes, at least, full of life, are taking over.

As women break their silence, they do so with extraordinary emotion and with unmistakable energy. So astonishing is it to the churches to hear the silent speak – rather like the moment in the film *One Flew Over the Cuckoo's Nest*, where the Red Indian chief breaks his catatonic silence with a remark about Juicy Fruit chewing gum – that so far they have been too surprised to notice that revolution is happening here and now. I suppose they may deal with it, as Fr Broadhurst would have them, by deciding that this upsurge of energy, this startling flow of water or issue of blood, right in the centre of the Church itself, shall be deemed heretical or unclean, and outlawed. I hope that won't happen because the great wealth of wisdom being offered, the wisdom of centuries of childbearing and cherishing, the wisdom of those who, whether they wish it or not, are intimately aware of the rhythm of

nature, the wisdom of those who have been forced to find
consolation in relationship since other consolations were
largely denied to them, seem breathtakingly relevant to a
world where relationship has broken down, where the
links between humanity and nature seem to have become
dangerously severed. It is not that women are superior to
men or even so very different – it is that their experience of
inferiority has, in the strange topsy-turvy processes of
God, begun to bear healing fruit. The stone that the
builders rejected is becoming the head of the corner.

Of course, women are not alone in this. As Harvey Cox
remarked some years ago:

> The main stimulus for the renewal of Christianity today
> is coming not from the center but from the bottom and
> from the edges. . . . It is coming from those places where
> Christians are poor, especially Latin America; from areas
> where they live as small minorities surrounded by non-
> Christian cultures, as they do in Asia; from the churches
> that live under political despotisms, as they have in the
> Communist world and in parts of South and Central
> America; from the American church of blacks and poor
> whites; from those women who are agonizing together
> over what it means to be Christian and female in a church
> that has perpetuated patriarchy for two millenia.[2]

What all these people have in common, Cox says, is that
they were pushed to the edges of Church and society into
basements, kitchens, slums and colonies. This banishment
left them innocent and somewhat ignorant of the patriarchal 'trip' because they were allowed no part in it, so that
now they come to the process of religious image-making
with a fresh version of Christianity that flies free of some of
the old inhibitions.

A question for those of us who have been shut out,
despised and silenced in the churches is why we should
continue to hang in there at all. Those who have read
Daphne Hampson's interesting book, *Theology and Feminism*,[3] will know that it is already being argued by her that

the churches are a fatal environment for women – that they
have not simply added to their burdens, but have been
among the principal architects of the persecuting
patriarchy. I think that there are important lessons to be
learned from Daphne's work, but feel closer to Rosemary
Radford Ruether's response that Daphne ignores the sense
of Christianity as an eschatological faith. In Rosemary's
words, 'it lives by the norm of the reign of God in the still
unrealized future of creation, not by a fixed, completed
past'. She suggests that this is the opposite of what she calls
Christian absolutism, which she defines as a belief that
'Christianity is the one true faith and that only through
Christian revelation, completed in one man two thousand
years ago, is there a true knowledge of God and redemption
from sin. All other religions are mere idolatry, if not
demonism.' She goes on to say that 'we need to recognize
the particularity of all religious traditions and their symbols
of relationship to the Divine. All are an integral part of
particular cultural communities and have shaped and been
shaped by their life and practice in these communities over
time ... all are particular ways of pointing to and experiencing eternal truth.' In contrast to Christian absolutism,
she experiences God as known in the midst of historical
struggle and change. There is a shattering of present reality
that makes way for change and growth and insight. 'One is
transported into a compelling experience of authentic divine justice in a way that reveals the utter hollowness of the
claims to divine righteousness made by such systems of
domination.' Such an experience, she suggests, is feminism. 'Feminist spirituality unmasks the claims of patriarchal religion to represent divine will. Women and men are
renewed in their authentic humanness and struggle against
patriarchal pretensions.' Such a faith sees God 'continually
breaking in from the future.'[4]

I hope that those most eager to promote the Decade of
Evangelism are similarly concerned with 'God breaking in
from the future', though I must confess I have my doubts.

Statements about it that I have read so far suggest something much more like a nostalgic return to a status quo that the speakers themselves found personally satisfying, but which some of us would find profoundly undesirable.

It is not that I am myself without some nostalgic longings, or even a considerable admiration for the extraordinary achievements of the Christian Church. It has been a remarkable container for a great deal that I value and that I believe to have been extremely valuable for humanity – for a rich culture that has fed us through art and music and architecture and literature and theatre, for pioneering work in medicine and psychology, in many kinds of therapy and social organization, in languages, in advanced philosophical and ethical debate, in cultural unities that extended across geographic barriers, in shared images and metaphors and jokes. For long periods of time it has been almost coterminous with European culture and civilization.

Yet some of these achievements, in the face of war, environmental disaster, and the painful confrontation with another great world religion whose fundamentalisms are no less frightening than our own, are not necessarily relevant to where we are now and may even hamper us in moving lightly and skilfully through the appalling complications of our situation.

I find that, as I think about God breaking in from the future, there are two images from the Christian past – at least one of which does not seem to me to have been adequately explored, and one that I want to hold on to.

The first of these is the image, depicted so often in paintings and icons and carvings and stained glass windows – perhaps more than any single Christian image – of the baby in its mother's arms, an image of relationship, of nurturing, of cherishing, of unity. Christian feminists, understandably, have difficulties with the person of the Virgin Mary, so often used to enjoin submission and humility upon women – not so much, as in the Annunciation story, submission and humility to the will of God, to which all Christians owe submission, as to a patriarchy that needs women to be inferior so that it may feel superior. The Virgin has also been used to force motherhood upon women who do not necessarily have such a vocation at all, and thus to deny that inner sense of autonomy and integrity which all true spirituality should be about. And finally she has been used, often by men who had small liking for actual flesh and blood women, to keep up a sort of proxy relationship to women, a sexuality once removed which made it possible perhaps to sublimate sexual feelings while eschewing what was deemed to be the contamination of female flesh – a very odd procedure.

Yet despite all those distorted uses of this great female archetype, I believe there is still something infinitely precious in the simple image of a baby in its mother's arms. Chartres Cathedral, that great hymn to the feminine, reaching unselfconsciously as it does back to the earth mothers who preceded Mary, of whom signs and symbols can be found all over Europe and some other parts of the world in the black madonnas, all speaking of a forgotten rootedness into nature, of the fundamental relationship between embryo and mother, of the first dependence, in feeding, embracing, cleaning, caring, experienced by every human being and reflecting the dependence of every human being upon the natural world that feeds us and upon God. It is this symbol, this picture of what I can only call a tenderness at the heart of things, however much we have degraded and distorted it, that has been and remains so potent at the heart of Christianity and which at last, I believe, can come into its own, as we learn to cherish femininity, and to cherish the earth as it has nurtured us. Cherish or perish is the lesson we must learn.

The other great Christian symbol that speaks most to me is the dreadful one of a man's body being stretched and torn upon a cross, the picture of Christ imitating human suffering. Here we see someone experiencing the uttermost in physical and psychological suffering. In its very simplicity it is a difficult symbol to understand, and it is widely misunderstood, by Christians as much as by anyone else, with its overtones of sadism and masochism, of punishment visited upon the innocent, of human resentment against a reputedly loving God who lets us suffer so unspeakably. I find it works for me not through intellectual understanding – I do not have the mental or the theological apparatus to make sense of what C.S. Lewis called 'The Problem of Pain' and I do not know who does – but through what I can only describe as recognition. Yes, I have seen that, with the baffling contradiction between God's love and human pain, yes I have been there, yes, if God is God then I need his or her participation and comprehension in this dark mystery.

As John Donne says in his 'Hymn to God the Father':

I have a sin of fear, that when I have spun
My last thread, I shall perish on the shore;
Swear by thyself, that at my death thy son
Shall shine as he shines now, and heretofore;
And having done that, Thou hast done,
I fear no more.[5]

Here and now, as we face the destruction of the planet, our faith is tried and tested in ways that we would once have found unimaginable. We are in a state of desperate danger and sickness, our survival hangs in the balance. At what perhaps is our death, the death of humanness, the death of this beautiful planet, it takes supreme faith to hope that Christ 'shall shine as he shines heretofore' and to make the act of trust and hope that means giving up our fear. Paradoxically it is that trust, that sense of standing in the love of God – God the father and God the mother – that may give us an outside chance of saving the situation. For it is fear, and the greed that fear spawns, that is at the heart of the sickness, and the only antidote to fear is love. Let us go back, and trace the pattern of God and humanity once more. Let us try to relearn the tune of the Hasid.

Notes

1 B.W. Harrison, *Feminist Theology – A Reader*, ed. A. Loades. London, SPCK, 1990, pp. 206–7.
2 H. Cox, 'Religion in the Secular City'. *Christian*, Summer 1986, p. 6.
3 D. Hampson, *Theology and Feminism*. Oxford, Basil Blackwell, 1990.
4 D. Hampson and R. Radford Ruether, 'Is There a Place for Feminists in the Christian Church?'. *New Blackfriars*, January 1987, pp. 8–9.
5 J. Donne, 'Hymn to God the Father', in *The Oxford Book of Christian Verse*. Oxford, Oxford University Press, 1940, p. 84.

CHAPTER EIGHT

Taking Responsibility

The Future of Christianity in Our Hands

HADDON WILLMER

CHOOSING IS INEVITABLE

Before 2020, we shall see the passing away of the remnants of the last generation in Britain who were Christians because they were brought up to feel that being Christian was respectable normality. Christianity will survive, if it does at all, because people choose to be Christian, in the full knowledge that there are other socially viable and intellectually attractive options. There will thus be a new Christian self-consciousness, as the practice of choosing permeates spirituality and church life. More and more Christians will become aware that being Christian today is close to what it is like to be a founder of a religion or at least of a religious movement: they will see themselves not as inheriting a given culturally well-rooted or even dominant religion, which could survive quite well if they never bothered with it, but as making a religion happen that would not be there if they and others did not actively choose it. They will experience a kind of responsibility for the future of faith that we can sense by contemplating what would have happened if Moses had refused the voice from the Burning Bush, or Paul had been disobedient to the heavenly vision, or Jesus had fallen to the tempter in the wilderness or come down from the cross. Founders and formers of religions hold the future of religions in their hands, though they rarely know it. They can let the future come through them or they can stifle it at its new birth. Deciding whether to be Christian or not today has these dimensions of awesome responsibility. It is to be a gatekeeper of the future. Or is this a grandiose misinterpretation of our situation?

Do we still need to argue that the future of Christianity is not ensured by its having been around a long time? Past endowments may pay for church buildings and pensions, but a living worthwhile faith always rests on the free-will offerings of people in the present.

Once there was a rough social truth and power in the following theologically dubious equation – to be Christian is to be Church of England, and to be Church of England is to be English. Its credibility always depended on taking a hard line with Dissenters, Protestant and Catholic, by persecuting or ignoring them. In the future, however, English ethnicity or nationalism will do little for Christianity; it is becoming hard to distinguish secularized nationalism and white ethnicity from racism and jingoism. In Wales, Scotland and Ireland, there is still a positive relation between some churches and some nationalisms, but even there nationalism is tending to be secularized and Christians are increasingly worried about the authenticity of any Christianity that uses it to recruit and rally support.

Nor will education do much for the future of Christianity. More has been expected from schools than they can now deliver. Those who made the 1944 Education Act accepted non-denominational Christianity as part of the national tradition into which children should be inducted; but the Act failed to produce that result, because of weakening conviction and an unwillingness to pay. The 1988 Education Act is unlikely to reverse the trend: that it wrote Christianity into the law so explicitly is a sign of weakness rather than strength. In the state system, religious education is required – but only by a flexibly administered, problematic law; and, worst of all, it is not recognized as a subject seriously short of teachers, even though there is no dispute that many who actually teach it have inadequate training or none at all for this extremely difficult subject. Furthermore, religious education has constantly been subverted by the need for moral socialization. It has been primarily concerned to awaken the religious sensibilities of children in a secular culture, while eliminating every trace of fanaticism. It seems to be implied that children will either belong to one religious tradition by virtue of their family upbringing or that they should be treated as eclectic consumers of religion according to personal taste; there is no expectation that religion is something for whose public communal future people might be educated to take responsibility. Religious education today is dominated by considerations of respect for individuals as choosers, but the choice is privatized and easily becomes trivial.

Christian habits are no longer consistently supported by social mores and media, customs and institutions. People from sociable open-air Caribbean islands tell me that they kept going to church because they could not hide from the extended family and observant neighbours. In Britain, a cold wet indoors society, religious habits lack such public support.

Christianity in the future will not reproduce itself simply by teaching children the faith, however well that is done. The Victorian era of Sunday schools is over. Upbringing in our society cannot produce unbreakable lifelong habits. Children will not grow up into Christ through growing up in Christian homes and in church, arriving by unbroken process and without crisis to adult Christianhood. Christian upbringing will not shield even small children from bewildering options. As a result, many who eventually become Christians, say in their twenties or later – an increasingly fashionable time for conversion – will have varied pilgrimages, often including periods of intentional rejection of Christianity and positive experimentation in other ways of life and faith. Some may come creatively and purposefully to Christianity, wanting to carry further what they have been experimenting with. Others will be seeking a new birth through the freedom to forget their pasts.

There will often be tension between these two sorts of future Christians, but they will have in common that they chose Christianity as adults, rather than being made Christian by upbringing. So the future of Christianity in Britain depends more than ever on evangelizing adults.

THE DENOMINATIONAL MANAGEMENT OF CHOICE

What kind of choice will be available in the future of Christianity in Britain? Imagine the future Christian as a customer in the religious supermarket of our rich society. Many brands are laid out on the shelves. There is choice, but the greatest part of the choosing has already been made by others: the manufacturers and the managers of the shop have decided what to display. Christians will become more self-conscious choosers in future, but what they have to choose from will, largely, be managed and arranged by various organizations, by mission agencies from the United States, and, above all, by churches.

In 2020, I think it likely (though of course in this mug's game I may well be proved wrong long before) that the main denominations as we know them now will still manage most of the shelf-space in the Christian section of the religious supermarket. This prospect causes me to swing between regret and gratitude; on balance, it is something to regret. Whether we like it or not, it means that taking responsibility for Christianity will generally involve working in, through or around denominations, on the terms that they set or permit to be negotiated. The burden of proof rests with those who expect a future for Christianity not organized by the denominations.

Thirty years ago, the Methodist ecumenical statesman and witty Luther scholar, Gordon Rupp, said that you cannot make ecumenical cement out of denominational marshmallow. Since then, as though they were following his advice, the denominations in Britain have been ensuring that whatever else they are made of, it is not marshmallow. The present situation might be described as a mattress of ecumenical marshmallow on which large and small rock-hard nuts of denominations sometimes dance in friendly unison – and sometimes collide painfully. In the present church scene the really powerful bodies are the denominations. They have the central organization and the extensive networks of local branches; they control money, patronage, and the formation and mobilization of Christians. The command structures and the officer corps of the Christian community are concentrated in the denominations.

Any analysis of the power structure of future British Christianity will note that church leaders rise through denominations. Within Christianity, there is no long-term career structure outside the denominations and bodies closely associated with them. The Christian leaders of thirty years' time are already being schooled and formed denominationally. Most training for the ministry is still organized denominationally. If, in 2020, there are to be leaders with many contacts and developed skills and wisdom, they will have to build them in a long apprenticeship starting now. People will not turn out to be leaders then unless there are denominational ladders they can climb step by step until they are mature – or should we say until they are denominationally domesticated? I admit it is increasingly likely that those who become leaders of denominations will have worked with other Christians on their way to the top, but the key to promotion will continue to be their personal and professional credibility within their own denomination.

This denominational distribution of power will shape the future. I therefore do not expect that, in thirty years' time, denominations will have disappeared. They will be friendly as they are now. But except in pockets where the local branches of the denominations are small and not likely to grow, they will maintain their separate identities.

The transition from the British Council of Churches to the Council of Churches for Britain and Ireland, and Churches Together in England and its fellow councils in Wales, Ireland and Scotland, does not promise a significant reduction in the power of denominations in the coming decades. It means that the denominations have brought ecumenism to heel. Ecumenical inter-church institutions are now relatively weaker than they were before 1990. The new structures ensure that they are dependent on the leaders of denominations for resources and authority. Many church leaders in Britain now covenant to do as much as they can together, but they still quote or adapt the 'Word to the Churches' of the Lund Faith and Order conference in 1952: 'Should not our churches ask themselves whether ... they should not act together in all matters except those in which deep differences of conviction compel them to act separately?'[1] Thus a powerful excuse for being unecumenical is embedded in pledges of ecumenical commitment. Our delicate ecumenisms depend on treading softly wherever any participant claims conscientious reasons for holding aloof. The general and proper respect for conscience makes it available for use as the last refuge of prejudice, to defend traditional denominational identity or interest against novel ecumenical possibility.

Even if ecumenism achieves more than this unhappy analysis suggests, it is virtually certain that in 2020 there will be many Churches, not one Church. The relative strengths of denominations and the patterns of relations between them may change. Adrian Hastings suggests, for example, that the episcopal churches, Roman Catholic and Anglican with some Methodists, may come closer together, but I doubt whether either the Roman Catholic Church or Church of England will give up anything essential to their separate organized identities.[2] In any case, this rearrangement would not achieve unity: other native or deeply rooted British churches, especially of a Baptist, charismatic and evangelical sort, will live by their own dynamic congregational and voluntaristic apprehension of the gospel, and they will break out of the episcopalian net every time it seems to be closing in on them. And it will be a good thing for British Christianity that they resist assimilation.

Even if church membership continues to decline (and it may not), the denominational control of Christianity is unlikely to disappear. The overall loss in numbers may be offset practically by increasing wealth and rationalized organization. In the last thirty years many small local churches have been closed, so that the denominations of the future are likely to have higher proportions of viable, confident congregations than they have done during the long decline that has for most of them been going on since around 1910. Their consciousness will not in future be so shaped by the gloom caught from watching old local churches dying slowly in public until they are made into warehouses, shrouded in carpets for sale or turned into desirable apartments. Individual local churches and congregations may not be so large as in the past, but, sharing in the affluence of Britain and using modern technology, they will support busy ministers and expensive apparatus and will be proud to do so. Churches will be made up increasingly of people for whom church is a local voluntary activity worth paying for. Denominations will gain buoyancy from congregations large and effective enough to make the minority of Christians feel cheerful about their prospects. Under such circumstances, even if secularization continues, there will be less pressure to give up denominational identity for the sake of united Christian survival.

LAY CHOICE OR LAY DOCILITY?

So far I have made two points: first, Christianity's future depends on increasingly self-conscious and deliberate choice and, secondly, the existing denominations will predominantly shape the choices open to those who want to choose Christianity.

These two points do not happily fit together. Where denominations manage choices, they may tend to obscure how radically Christianity depends on choice. Churches rely upon people to choose church and Christianity, but, after the initial choice is made, they tend to prefer people to stick faithfully, to form a steady habit of loyalty. Then churches can commend themselves as the end of people's spiritual wanderings in which they find relief from the burden of choice. And many are ready to be grateful to churches for defining choices, bringing some order to an otherwise confusing range of possibilities, and preventing religious anomie and disorientation. Many people want manageable choices. They see virtue in escaping egotistic individualism and spiritual anarchy. These days, as much or more than ever, they prefer to have their religion without being taken to the borders of madness, where the mind cracks at the infinite unmanageability of mystery. Consequently, there is a danger that churches – including charismatic ones – will build their futures on the docile support of those who want to be relieved of taking responsibility for the future of Christianity – or indeed of anything else. The result may be churches that only dull and unadventurous people can endure.

Churches often feel it is pastorally justified to define, manage and minimize choices. The ambiguity of such pastoral caring was exposed, long ago, by Dostoevsky in his story of Christ being brought before the Grand Inquisitor: the authoritative hierarchy gives people the bread and security they crave, and so cannot tolerate Christ who insists impractically on calling them to freedom. I wonder whether this story will bite as sharply into church consciousness in 2020 as it did in and after 1920.

If many people are docile, churches in the future may depend excessively on the choice of the clergy (or their equivalents), on the tiny minority of those who venture their lives for a church by making it their profession. By making promises and becoming part of the institution through ordination, clergy are people who publicly choose the future of some form of Christianity as their own personal career. They are different from other people, whose work for the future of Christianity need be little more than a leisure choice, to be abandoned when it is no longer fun. The lay choice of Christianity may be sincere and profoundly personal, but it does not take up our life's working time, in which we tend to spend our best energies; nor are laypeople dependent on the Church for their bread and butter, their social status or their self-respect as workers.

It will be a major need of future Christianity to do more than has yet been done, despite much talk, to show that genuinely lay modes of life, in and out of the institutional Church, can be given public recognition as ways of taking effective responsibility for the future of Christianity. Until that is achieved we will continue in the old rut: the lay task, however attractively packaged, will tend to be concretized in paying for the clergy and supporting them in what they do. A powerful critique of this unsatisfactory division of duties is to be found in Rabbi Dow Marmur's *Beyond Survival*.[3] This analysis of questions faced by Judaism in Britain could easily be borrowed by Christians trying to understand their own situation. A religion may indeed survive in some form so long as it pays its clergy but, he asks, what is such survival worth? What can survival mean for a religion unless there are better reasons to survive than merely surviving?

A great issue, therefore, for the future is whether we will get beyond the respectable theology of the laity, to the genuine realization of lay Christianity, so that in 2020 churches are really less clericalist than they are now. The Anglican report, *All are Called*, says: 'In this generation the Church is more and more losing the character of an institution and taking on that of a movement.'[4] Whether this is so, and whether it will come to much, depends on unclericalized laypeople, taking an intelligent, lifelong responsibility for moving Christianity onwards. It is not enough for them to be private Christians for merely personal, even religiously consumerist, reasons while leaving the future of Christianity to the clergy, who stand out as odd persons because they have institutionally promised their future to the service of the institutional future of Christianity. There are indeed signs that lay groups and initiatives are burgeoning. They use denominations selectively and sit loose to them when they do not seem helpful. These lay movements, however, rarely confront the denominational and largely clerical structures; they prefer to outflank them. Since, on this view, they have neither broken with denominations nor transformed them, they are still vulnerable to the frustration with church structures that is a widespread characteristic of contemporary Christianity. Lay Christianity will, I expect, continue to oscillate between skilful exploitation of ecclesiastical resources and indecisive alienation from the churches. Being creative lay Christians in touch with the Church will be as difficult as ever.

What we need for the future are churches that encourage choosers and do not conceal the truth that churches depend on daily renewed choice by all their members. What matters is the quality, the relevance, the criteria and implementation of choice. But such responsible churches will not happen unless the kinds of Christianity that refuse to take responsibility for the future are confronted. I have said enough about ecclesiastical docility, which may be laziness masked by the comfort of dependent piety. Now I turn to the grand objection concerning taking responsibility for the future of Christianity, which arises, it could be argued, from the gospel itself. Simply, that it is actually unchristian to be concerned about the future of Christianity.

LEAVE THE FUTURE TO GOD!

To take responsibility for making the future – is that not to show that we do not really trust God, but instead want to take his place? Is it not a sign that the Church has succumbed implicitly to modern humanism, or atheism – in other words, there is no God who can and does determine the course of events in this world, so human beings are left to take up the task?

Whatever else happens to Christianity, if it is to deserve respect, its heart of honest and intelligent faith in God, genuine reverential trust and submission to God, must be in good health. If Christians are theologically serious in this way, are they not required to leave the future to God, to do their immediate duty, to love mercy, to seek justice and to walk humbly with God? Little people – as we all are – should act day by day, doing the best they can in the little circle of candlelight given to them, without seeing far into the future or making calculations about it. If they do what they can, God will bring out of, or impose upon, their efforts whatever future is his gift and his judgement. That seems to be the obviously Christian spirit. It is certainly traditionally thought to be so. And it opposes the spirit of modern planning which in many areas, like the arms industry, thinks twenty or thirty years ahead.

The Sermon on the Mount can be expected to be part of the future of Christianity; it has repeatedly disturbed customary Western Christianity in this century and I trust it will do so again. It calls for perfection modelled on the Father in heaven, ethics without compromise, faith in God without anxiety, openness of being without hypocritical exhibitionism, love of enemies. It presents Jesus as saying among other things: 'Do not be anxious about tomorrow, for tomorrow will be anxious for itself' (Matt. 6.34). If we are not to worry about where tomorrow's food and clothing is to come from, it is even less permissible for us to be troubled about the future of Christianity. Can we not leave that to God? After all, is it not his business? When thinking of the future, do we not need to heed Gamaliel's advice (Acts 5. 38,39)? 'If . . . this undertaking [the early development of what was becoming Christianity in Jerusalem] is of men, it will fail; but if it is of God, you will not be able to overthrow [it].'

Even if we take the words of Jesus as they stand, we could argue thus: we are indeed not to be anxious about tomorrow, the time hidden from us, which we can do nothing about. Today is the time when we can and must be responsible, dealing with whatever is within our reach, open to being affected and influenced by us in some measure. Today is made up very largely, however, of the possibility and the seeds of tomorrow: there are many things we can do today that will not bear fruit immediately, but may do so tomorrow. Today is full not of tomorrow as tomorrow, but of the todayness of tomorrow. But the todayness of tomorrow – which is today's responsibility – will never happen in tomorrow's time, if we do not prepare the way for it today. None of us lives in a futureless present in matters we care about – we all hope and plan – and, to use a superficial interpretation of this saying to excuse indifference to the future of Christianity would merely show that Christianity is not important for us. Jesus also told the parable about the poor man who hid his talent in the ground because he did not want to face the future: he should at least have put his money in the local building society. Jesus did not teach that the present is a self-enclosed and self-sufficient moment. Look carefully at today and you will see it is full of tomorrow.

An argument of this sort may be a help but it does not settle the matter. Whether taking responsibility for the future of Christianity is compatible with faith in and obedience to God as revealed in Jesus Christ, cannot be made to turn on a single text like Matthew 6.34. Deciding this issue involves a comprehensive reckoning with the Christian faith as a whole carried out from its own centre. What is to be found at the centre of Christianity? There are many ways of pointing to it; I can try only one here.

THE FUTURE OF GOD IN HUMAN HANDS

Most forms of Christianity believe that God is not God without humanity since God took humanity upon himself and became human in Jesus Christ. This humanity of God is interpreted and lived in many different ways, with a variety of implications for human responsibility. A systematic analysis of all these ways is impossible here; I want to highlight that sort of interpretation of incarnation that loads human beings with awesome responsibility, which, for God's sake, should not be refused. The first step is to remember that the incarnation of God in Jesus is not to be regarded merely as a single secluded event, a special privileging of one man over against all others, but rather as the pivotal revelation, realized in one person, of the relation God intends and seeks to have with all humanity. Incarnation means that God chooses to be intimately related to humanity, through flesh and blood, in historic community. God's oneness with humanity is not merely a triumphant transformation of humanity, empowering and raising it by divine indwelling to a level beyond itself. That might be read as closer to the abolition of humanity than the affirmation of it. Instead, God is united with human being by becoming as vulnerable to human beings as human beings in general are.

This is one reason why the actual story of Jesus seems to me to be so important. There God is one with human beings not ideally but actually, by being in the hands of human beings, at their disposal, from the cradle to the cross. One of the central but most overlooked ways in which God shares human vulnerability and is in human hands is that Jesus was and is talked about, interpreted in an endless variety of ways. That is to say, others decide who he is and what he counts for. There is no way by which we can avoid responsibility in this process of interpreting Jesus, which will last, so some Christians say, until he is revealed in the coming glory. Meantime, he is there to be talked about and, if you wish, to be laughed at – or with.

On a broadly Christian reading, the essential intention of the action of God in Christ is to reconcile humanity to God, by saving humanity from its failure to be human. Human beings fail to be human partly because they so often refuse or misuse the natural responsibility that God the Creator puts into their hands. By incarnation, God reaffirms that delegation of responsibility to human beings, by making it clear that their responsibility is more extensive than was often believed and that the past failures to be responsible do not mean that people are now relieved of responsibility.

The incarnation of God in Jesus Christ shows that human beings are not merely responsible for themselves, or for whatever part of the creation lies within their ever-growing power, but also for God. In Jesus Christ, so Christians believe – and all that is being argued here is that Christians should make the future out of faithfulness to what they can discern is given them in Christian faith – God became human and, from the cradle to the cross, God is here in human hands.

God, then, has made the future of God a human responsibility. If that is so, Christians cannot use submission to God as an excuse for not taking responsibility for the future. Submitting to God means accepting God's gift of the life of responsible choice. Now, it would be paradoxical if believers were encouraged and required by their faith to take responsibility for the future of God, humanity and global creation, only to be exempted from responsibility for the future of that faith itself.

Clearly, there is great danger to Christianity from this kind of interpretation of incarnation. Christianity has stressed that the substance of faith is the gift of God. It is not a human work, creation or choice. Faith is hopeful and helpful because in it we are found by God and are released from the instability and disasters of our own makings of life, our self-making, individual and corporate. While we may claim limited freedom over against other creatures, when faced with God we come to the place where we must surrender our attempts to master ourselves, for here we meet the Giver and the Judge, in whom we live and move and have our being. Here we come to the point where it is not our choice, but properly the choice of another that defines and guards our being. So self-surrender, and the readiness to be determined by grace, come into play. Christianity will disappear in the future if it loses this sense of determining grace, which is the sense of God. It will also disappear if it denies the importance of choice, including the way in which our choosing shapes the Christianity that is available for us.

149

A solution to this little problem is already implicit in the account I have offered of the centre of Christian faith. God is Lord and yet chooses to be shaped in and through human choices. We are indeed not to make idols, false Gods: we are not to take that which is not God and treat it as God. But the true God gives himself to human beings to be made something of, to be born and cared for, to be listened to and misunderstood, to be praised for his wonderful and mighty deeds, to be despised and rejected. God is in human hands, the work and victim of human choosings, the responsibility of human beings. To make religiously creative choices, to take responsibility for human being (and even for Christianity?) is not to deny the sovereign choice of God that determines us, but it is to go along the way determined for us by the God who made himself our responsibility by putting himself in our hands. God indeed puts himself into human hands to be born, murdered, interpreted. But in that life and death, God becomes arrestingly present to people: they are surprised that the One they dispose of shapes them as Lord. At the cross the centurion in charge of the killing process witnesses: This was a good man; this was the Son of God. It is as we take responsibility for shaping Christianity at its centre, as faith in God as he is in Jesus, that it may be given us to find and to see that we are being shaped, that the Other finally takes responsibility for us.

WHY CHOOSE CHRISTIANITY?

Taking responsibility for the future is not then contrary to Christian faith in God, but rather is the path given us by God's grace along which we find grace. But now we cannot avoid the question of the relation between Christian responsibility for the divine-human future and responsibility for the future of this specific, historical religion, Christianity. Are even Christians to give a privileged status to the future of Christianity? Why choose Christianity rather than other possibilities for life? There are theological reasons for not devoting ourselves to the future of a particular human religion, especially if it is our own. Yet, as I have argued, if there is to be any future for Christianity, it must be chosen and worked for: and that means that people must be persuaded that it has such worth in itself as to win the service of their lives in preference to other claims. But how can Christianity be shown to have this kind of worth without making claims to uniqueness and ultimacy that have become hard to sustain in mixed company?

Christianity in the next thirty years will continue to be pressed by the question whether in a world like ours being Christian ought to have priority for any of us. Few British Christians now seriously believe, whatever they say, that Christian believing is a condition of eternal salvation. And those who see that being human involves taking responsibility for the future will be inclined to think that it is far more urgent to work for the survival of the globe and of endangered species, for justice and international peace, for the socializing of capitalism and the humanizing of our cities, for the maintenance of the National Health Service and even of the university than for the future of Christianity. Are these urgent claims in competition with one another? At a physical and individual level, they are: we all have limited energy, time and vision. No-one can do everything. Many people do not make a positive decision *against* Christianity, but they will do little for its future because they are working for other causes. At a spiritual intellectual level, however, these concerns need not be in competition. Christianity, least of all, needs to be in competition with them provided it develops itself as a faith that comes to expression and works itself out in taking responsibility for the future, in prayer and righteous action, as Bonhoeffer put it, knowing that God is there for us to honour and serve in the neighbour, the poor and all of the world which is at human disposal.[5] The future of God is at stake in what human beings do about all these matters that are his creation and concern. Genuine Christianity consists in caring about God's future in them all, not in securing the future of one religion against the world. Theological and spiritual conflict within the churches on this issue will continue to be as painful as it is unavoidable.

Christianity has to find its future in taking responsibility for the human future and the world's future: it is called to find itself in hoping and suffering and striving with the world. That means that as a religion, it has to exist perpetually on the edge of disappearing into practical human concerns, or humanism, as some call it. Christianity must be and must remain precarious as an historical religion if it wishes to be true and responsible to its calling. True Christianity is a faith with the courage to be humanist.

CARRYING THE STORY OF JESUS

How can Christianity develop in a non-competitive mode, serving the future of God in the human future, without losing its identity, and falling apart through self-neglect? The only viable way, I think, lies in its relation with Jesus.

Christianity carries the story of Jesus: that is above all what it has to offer and why I hope it will survive. Christianity carries, but does not possess, this story, as it would do if it perfectly lived the story while no-one else even listened to it. Jesus and his story are not identical with the community of Christians. Nevertheless, the Christian community has a special relation with the story: it tells this story repeatedly, attends to it, bears it in many different ways. Outside Christian communities, many are interested in the story of Jesus and often make much of it, but its survival as a story of accumulating significance will, as ever, depend on communities that dedicate themselves to the ever-renewed tellings, hearings and performances of the story.

The future of Christianity is a theological task partly because there is no simple relation between Christian communities and the story of Jesus. Too often, scholarship separates study of the story from the communities and their active responsibility for the future. Too often, the communities place themselves brashly at the centre of the continuing story of Jesus, so that the Church is virtually identified with Christ. Christians, however, can be in the story of Jesus only as the disciples who followed him to the place of crucifixion where 'they stood at a distance and saw these things' (Luke 23.49). The Church carries the story of Jesus as the story of its watching this Other with whom it never manages to be identical. This story of Jesus is the judgement of the Church: it knows itself in its unfaithfulness and its falling short, for it does not get crucified with him, but manages only to keep on watching from a distance. Thanks to the story of Jesus, which does not allow the Church to identify itself with the One it cannot escape, Christianity is necessarily a self-critical religion. It is self-critical not primarily because it has (rightly) been ready to learn from the Enlightenment, but because it carries the story of Jesus. In a future when touchy, fearful and aggressive fundamentalisms will flourish, it is important that Christianity continues to be a positively chosen but highly self-critical religion. And that depends on its standing at the cross and watching, albeit from a long way off.

Let me sum up with a wish for the future of Christian festivals, as I look for a change in the way Christianity images itself in our culture. I hope that in 2020 Christianity in Britain will have come to make little or nothing of the nativity and Christmas, whose commercialism, nostalgia and sentimentality about God and humanity lead us into annual bouts of misrepresenting Christian faith with the false hope that Christianity can be built on keeping children happy. Pentecost will only be an improvement on Christmas as the central Christian festival, if it is purged of the triumphalism, manipulation and unrealism that now so often beset it. It is rather to be hoped that by 2020, we will be close enough to the centre of gravity of responsible Christian faith to be able to watch at Good Friday, where the spring of new creation is compressed.

NOTES

1 O.S. Tomkins ed., *The Third World Conference on Faith and Order*. London, SCM, 1953, p. 16. The Covenant between the Church leaders in West Yorkshire includes a commitment to do everything together, 'except that which, in conscience, must be done separately'. I am told that ecumenical covenants made in other places mention 'church polity' as a permissible reason for acting separately; that makes quite explicit the reality of denominational inhibition.

2 A. Hastings, *A History of English Christianity 1920–1985*. London, Collins, 1986, p. 668.

3 D. Marmur, *Beyond Survival*. London, DLT, 1982, pp. 44–50: 'The quest for survival, in itself legitimate, noble and necessary has led many Jews into expecting others to do the surviving for them.'

4 General Synod Board of Education, *All Are Called: Towards a Theology of the Laity*. London, CIO Publishing, 1985, p. v.

5 D. Bonhoeffer 'Thoughts on the Baptism of D.W.R.' in *Letters and Papers from Prison*. London, Fontana, 1959, p. 160: 'pray and do right and wait for God's own time'.